LEADING CHANGE IN TURBULENT TIMES

HOW EFFECTIVE LEADERS EXECUTE CHANGE AND LAND SAFELY IN HEALTH AND BUSINESS

MICHAEL S. LAWSON, MBA

authorHOUSE®

AuthorHouse™
1663 Liberty Drive
Bloomington, IN 47403
www.authorhouse.com
Phone: 1-800-839-8640

First published by AuthorHouse 12/8/2010

ISBN: 978-1-4520-9290-4 (sc)
ISBN: 978-1-4520-9291-1 (e)
ISBN: 978-1-4520-9289-8 (dj)

Library of Congress Control Number: 2010915744

Printed in the United States of America

CONTENTS

PREFACE

"Go confidently in the direction of your dreams. Live the life you've imagined." —Henry David Thoreau

This book is for Americans who want to improve their lives; the corporation that is preparing for or preventing turbulent times; the CEO who is leading a turnaround of his or her company; and the health care executives that are preparing for upcoming health care reform.

Creating a purpose and direction in life, no matter if it is a corporation or individual, is essential. I developed my own personal mission statement more than twenty-five years ago when I was a senior in high school. It stated, "I want to improve my health, increase my wealth, and expand my knowledge." My rationale for explaining the mission began with the view that the first priority was health because without health, nothing was important.

Second, having the financial wherewithal to generate revenue to meet basic human needs is essential; therefore wealth would allow me to support my family, my friends, and myself. Finally God gave us all the ability to learn; therefore knowledge was the key to sustaining health, increasing wealth, and learning to change and advance in life.

Life has taught me that change is constant, and you must be prepared to stay committed to your mission through personal leadership and adaptability in a turbulent environment. In our American history, health and economic crises continue to occur in life, resulting in economic recessions, loss of life, and opportunities to recover.

We must be prepared to deal with these challenges. This book is about being more prepared to effectively lead change and to adapt in turbulent times in personal and corporate health as well as organizational development and transformation. The goal is to land safely and be stronger in order to handle change in the future.

I dedicate this book to my late beloved brother, Gerald Lawson Jr.; my grandmothers, Rose Withers-Washington and Evelyn Lawson, my grandfather Lloyd Washington; and my mother Alberta Washington-Miles. They demonstrated a passion for serving and loving others during turbulent times in their life.

They served the customers of General Motors, Cleveland Clinic, and Huron Hospital of Ohio with everlasting commitment to service excellence while providing for their families and loving others during turbulent times related to their own health. What was great was that you would have never known about their problems because they always smiled and exemplified love to everyone despite their conditions.

My grandmothers died of cancer and brother died of diabetes, and heart disease. These experiences challenged them in ways others will not experience until it is their time. They all showed personal leadership by setting a goal to fight these dreadful diseases through seeking treatment and education. They wanted to save and prolong their lives, which allowed them to stay focused on their mission to serve others and love their family.

This book also shares a blueprint on how Americans and corporations adapt, face challenges head-on, and solve problems experienced in difficult times. The problems can range from health decline to fighting for equal rights and stopping the mounting financial losses of a corporation.

Challenges occur in life relative to health, careers, relationships, and business. It is important to sense the development of these challenges because unfavorable trends can emerge, and a turbulent crisis may develop and require leadership in order to improve. Some may ask what I mean by turbulent. The Oxford dictionary defines turbulent as an irregular or stormy condition.

"Irregularity or stormy" could mean disturbing upheaval in a person's health such as heart attack, diabetes, or cancer. It can also mean loss of a job or a noticeable decline in an organization's financial performance due to the economy, poor management, or competitors entering the markets.

Americans are experiencing stormy or disturbing conditions in their health and jobs, resulting in unemployment and death. In 2009 America experienced a recession as well as a health crisis. We were in one of the longest recessions since World War II. The Trading Economics reported that the recession started in 2008 and continued into 2010 with a total of more than 14.6 million people unemployed. The unemployment rate in August 2010 was 9.5percent; the normal unemployment rate is typically around 5 percent.

There are even more people affected by the health crisis. Chronic disease is a major health concern and accounts for approximately 75 percent of total health care expenditures. Two of the chronic diseases, heart disease and cancer, are the leading causes of death in the United States. Other chronic diseases such as diabetes and kidney disease are appearing in mind-boggling numbers. More than twenty-six million Americans have kidney disease, and more than twenty-four million have diabetes. Another fifty-seven million Americans have pre-diabetes. These statistics clearly indicate emerging trends that require a turnaround by strong leadership with an emergency crisis plan.

CHAPTER ONE

EMERGENCY PLANNING FRAMEWORK

"The art of progress is to preserve order amid change and to preserve change amid order." —Alfred Whitehead

One thing that is guaranteed in life is constant change; therefore we should always expect the unexpected and be prepared for any emergency that may occur related to our organizations, jobs, family, financial situation, or health. We never know which situation may occur, however I guarantee an emergency will happen.

Emergencies are part of our ongoing journey in life. It may be a minor emergency or a major crisis regardless of the severity, a structure and plan should be in place to manage the turbulent situation. Without a plan and structure, fragmented and uncoordinated efforts may occur, resulting in time loss, resources untapped, and a recurring problem.

An emergency or crisis could be mounting financial losses, unemployment, closure of a business, divorce, or loss of a life. An emergency plan must have a framework in order to respond and manage the crisis. The following should be executed and in place:

- The leader must authorize the implementation of the emergency plan and develop a team.

1

- The crisis, emergency, or turbulent situation must be announced.
- The current status must be communicated and a plan developed.
- An emergency plan specific to the situation must be identified.
- The leader should assign an emergency action plan opened and a turnaround command leader.
- An information officer must develop a team and a communication plan.
- Actions must first ensure health and safety of self, personnel, family, or organization.
- The leader should assign liaison responsibility in order to deal with employees, family, and agencies.
- The leader should assign an operations leader to begin emergency operations and the turnaround plan.
- Time frames must be established to regroup and report status updates.
- Status updates must be documented and used for interventions and education.
- Plans must continue to be executed until the situation is resolved and turned around.

TURNAROUND MANAGEMENT IN HEALTH AND BUSINESS

"Organizational change begins with leaders who walk the talk by transforming themselves." —Stratford Sherman

A turnaround can involve an individual or corporation experiencing turbulent times in which some type of disaster must be prevented or stopped. Has there ever been a time in your life when you knew it was time for a change? You or your organization may have experienced a death in the family, a loss of job(s), mounting financial losses, ongoing stressful problems in a relationship, or unhealthy habits affecting health.

There are people who develop bad habits such as overeating, smoking, drinking, or excessive debt. These habits can lead to numerous problems—obesity and diabetes, lung cancer and heart disease, liver disease and pancreatic cancer, or even divorce and bankruptcy.

Even corporations develop unfavorable habits and cultures that lead to over hiring, autocratic management style, poor strategic policy execution, untimely product and service delivery, and high levels of debt. The outcomes of these ways of practice lead to very high labor expense ratios, overly controlling management, low employee morale, increasing financial losses, and declines in market share.

Regardless whether the situation applies to an individual or a corporation, evidence shows a turnaround is necessary. People have stopped smoking, lost more than one hundred pounds, lowered their blood pressure, and even beat cancer. Corporations have reorganized their excessively layered structures, thereby reducing the staff and expense base; introduced new products, which increased revenue; and established new cultures that improved employee morale, service delivery, and customer satisfaction.

Now it is time for you to take the lead in these turbulent times in order to begin the turnaround management process. It begins with a transition process that includes a macro- and microanalysis of the targeted individual or organization, and it develops into the creation of an initial turnaround plan.

In the transition process there are three objectives that must be achieved:

1. Identify stakeholders who will be crucial to the turnaround
2. Obtain and review all relevant and accurate data to understand the person or organization
3. Set up interviews, meetings, and evaluations to identify areas that need immediate attention

It is also important to establish a task force or team of people and clearly communicate purpose, scope of responsibility, specific objectives, needs, and assignments to the team. This team can provide a report of the structure and performance metrics, a diagnosis of problems, current mitigations, and future recommendations for turnaround.

Before recommendations can be suggested, there first must be an understanding of the symptoms. For example, the following habitual signs and symptoms can contribute to chronic diseases such as heart and kidney diseases, cancer, and diabetes.

- Smoking
- Blurred vision, weight loss, abrupt fatigue, dehydration
- Untreated blood pressure higher than 130/90 for extended period of time

- Aerobic exercise less than 3 days per week and 30 minutes per day
- High consumption of saturated fat and sugar
- Total cholesterol > 200, LDL > 130, HDL > 45, and Triglycerides > 200
- Daily alcohol consumption exceeding two drinks
- Body mass index (BMI) of 25 or higher

Sustaining a healthy ideal body weight can prevent chronic diseases and prevent the need for a weight reduction turnaround plan. The table below shows the classifications and ideal body mass index.

Classifications	Body Mass Index
Underweight	Less than 18.5
Normal	18.5 to 24.9
Overweight	25 to 29.9
Obesity class 1	30 to 34.9
Obesity class 2	35 to 39.9
Obesity class 3	Greater than 40

CHAPTER TWO

HEALTH CRISIS AND PROTEIN DIET IMPACT

"Example is a contagious behavior." —Charles Reade, English novelist

Some may ask how can we regain an ideal BMI, reduce blood cholesterol, eliminate heart disease, and prevent chronic diseases such as cancer and diabetes. It can start with the food that is put in your body. A best seller called *The China Study: T. Colin, Cambell, PhD. The China Study, Banbella Books Publisher, 2006, page 115*, reported that American men's death rate of coronary heart disease was seventeen times higher than rural Chinese men.

The study also reported on page 73 that 80 percent of American protein consumption came from animal-based foods, whereas in China only 10 percent came from animal-based foods. China reported lower rates of chronic diseases and cancers. There are several chemicals that can help cause cancer. For example, the meat preservative called nitrite, the human carcinogen called nitrosamines, and the fungal toxin called aflatoxin all contribute to cancer development.

Aflatoxin can help initiate tumors by entering cells and being metabolized by enzymes, which then forms dangerous products that target cells, damage DNA, and possibly multiply. This process occurred in liver cancer cases. Animal-based protein intake can initiate the enzyme related to aflatoxin metabolism.

The emphasis of *The China Study* is to consume plant-based proteins and reduce or eliminate animal-based proteins.

Red meat, fish, milk, cheese, yogurt, and eggs are considered animal proteins that help develop the following diseases:

- Breast cancer
- Liver cancer
- Colon cancer
- Leukemia
- Prostate cancer
- Heart disease
- Kidney stones
- Eye disease
- Brain disease
- Diabetes
- Osteoporosis (increases acid load and decreases calcium in bones)

Low-protein, plant-based diets can prevent and inhibit the growth of cancer and other chronic diseases. More specific, plant-based diets can lower blood cholesterol and decrease rates of various cancers and heart disease. For example, an eighteen patient heart disease study from world renown surgeon Caldwell B. Esselstyn Jr. proved that , plant-based diet can reduce LDL blood cholesterol levels, decrease coronary events, open arteries, and reverse heart disease.

In turbulent times related to health crisis, consuming plant-based foods can help save lives and transform lifestyles. The foods below are examples of plant-based diets:

- Colored vegetables: broccoli, spinach, lettuce, greens, cauliflower, cabbage, etc.
- Legumes: kidney beans, lentils, green beans, black beans, soy beans, etc.
- Roots: Carrots, potatoes, beets, onions, leeks, garlic, etc.
- Fruits: blueberries, peaches, oranges, strawberries, kiwi, apples, papaya, etc.
- Fiber and whole-wheat grains

- Mushrooms
- Nuts

Changing your food choices from animal-based to plant-based will contribute to a turnaround in your health that can help prolong your life and overcome chronic diseases. Human life is the most valuable asset, and one should take immediate action when necessary.

In a turnaround there must be a sense of urgency established, and you must know what is driving the mind to make inappropriate decisions, develop bad habits, and influence behavior to take wrong actions. If the turnaround is related to resolving preventable health problems, there is a sense of urgency to take actions that include the following:

- Identification and elimination of root cause bad habits
- Consolidation and reallocation of unproductive time
- Expansion and creation of alternative good habits: exercise, healthy plant food
- Decision to get diagnosed and receive medical treatment

These changes are critical to personal improvement and survival of the human body.

EMERGING TRENDS

> **"You always look where there's change. Change is what creates opportunity." —Gary Wendt**

Having the foresight to identify emerging trends in health or business can help you to better manage and effectively lead change in turbulent times. Foresight is related to understanding the trends. Some ways to increase foresight capabilities and identify emerging trends include the items listed below:

- Establish a credible information source and system to better detect patterns
- Assign a skilled and unified team to collect ground-level intelligence
- Create a culture of information sharing and learning
- Understand and use key indicators to determine signs of trends

- Demonstrate leadership and make proactive decisions to prepare for changes

Early warning signs are indicators that inform you change is coming, and it is best to have a strategy and be well positioned to weather the storm of change when it comes. The signs of change can be related to growth or decline in jobs, cash reserves and savings, consumer spending, debt, sales, chronic disease incident and mortality rates, obesity, , and noticeable patterns of behaviors.

During a recession or health crisis, indicators can be related to corporations or people; therefore understanding and preparing for the trends and creating solutions are critical to recovery and succeed. A recession can result in declining sales revenue, so it is wise to notice if sales show a trend of declining three to six consecutive months.

Turbulent economic times can result in job losses, and people may delay (or forego) going to the hospital. These unfortunate events can result in an increased unemployment rate exceeding 10 percent and high incident and mortality rates in chronic diseases. The increased health crisis requires new skill development for new jobs and wellness, as well as health coverage and disease management intervention to save lives. The economic recession and health crisis indicator below provides listing of problem indicators affecting a corporation or individual. Solutions are provided to address the problems and trends are listed to offer insight and activate action.

ECONOMIC RECESSION AND HEALTH CRISIS INDICATOR TABLE

Indicator	Corporation	People	Solutions	Trends
Sales/Revenue Decline	Lower than previous year	Income loss or stagnant	Innovation, pricing strategy, second jobs	Decline 3–6 months
Unemployment	Layoffs due to sales decline and need to reduce cost	Losing jobs at alarming rate	Entrepreneur, develop new skills, or seek employment	Typically 4–5% but increased to > 9%
Cash Reserves	Typically less than 100 days	Less than 3 months	Liquidate noncore assets	Typically 120–200 days but declined to < 60–90 days

Spending/Debt	Increasing at rate higher than revenue	Increasing at rate higher than income	Reduce	% spending increase > % revenue increase
Investing	High risk, lack diversity, declining value	Minimal to none	Bonds and guaranteed saving account	Continued DOW decline below 7,000
Construction or New Homes	Declining or stalled	Normally none	Delay until recession ends	Declining economy
Health Coverage	Declining and shifting to employees	Lost due to unemployment	Seek employment	Job loss increases
Incident and Mortality Rate	Impacting hospitals and cost of health care	Increasing due to chronic diseases, no PCP and delaying care	Wellness, education, PCP, and disease management	Increases in obesity, smoking, and lack of exercise
Loans	Stalled due to banks resisting	Declined due to credit scores	Reduce debt improve scores	Late payments, increased debt
Interest Rates	Declining to stimulate economy	Declining to stimulate consumer spending	Use low rates to acquire appreciating assets	Consumer spending decrease and unemployment
Debt, Business Close or Foreclosure	Increasing due to no cash to operate	Increasing due job loss and variable rates	Acquire	Job loss and declining cash reserves

BEHAVIORAL PATTERNS

In the book *Seeing What's Next,* Clayton M. Christensen said "the historian in us cares about the past and the decision maker in us cares about the future." This quote is very true relative to business, health historical facts, and patterns of behaviors.

I have learned about the past, and now I am preparing for the future predicated on key factual correlations related to three deceased male family members. I did not realize these correlations until my brother past away in May 2009. There was a similarity related to my forty-six-year-old brother, the 2004 death of my thirty-four-year-old cousin, and my fifty-two-year-old uncle's death in 2008. All three men unexpectedly died at relatively young ages.

They were smokers and diabetics, were hypertensive, drank alcohol, and were considered obese with BMI's exceeding thirty. The final two similarities were that they did not exercise, and all three of them died of heart attacks. The patterns of behavioral choices and co-morbid chronic diseases led to the heart attacks.

As I reflect on these last five years, I saw trends emerging in their earlier years of life that led to their health problems. After high school, they spent time with friends who enjoyed smoking and drinking, they never valued reading and education related to the importance of nutrition, and they did not exercise during the last ten to fifteen years of their lives.

As these unhealthy habits developed over time, signs of health problems began to appear when they were in their twenties, thirties, and forties. I noticed the emergence of these unhealthy trends and spoke to them about the importance of changing their lifestyle, but I never thought they would die at such young ages. These disruptive behaviors led to their demise but also to my awakening.

I realized this was my opportunity to innovate and demonstrate personal leadership and change by first leading by example, making changes in my life as well as encouraging others. Due to the deaths of my grandmother, brother, and other family members, I am an eleven-year vegetarian, do not smoke, and remain committed to exercising and sharing knowledge with others.

There are many American families mourning the loss of their loved ones due to similar situations. We must be passionately dedicated to wellness and encourage our family, friends, and communities to do the same. There is a sense of urgency, and now is the time to identify these unhealthy behaviors in teenagers, young adults, and even older people who are developing unhealthy habits. We can help them reverse these trends by sharing our stories, providing pathways to better choices and access to medical care, and ensuring constant follow-up. These methods are applied in business and can also be used in your personal life.

ENVIRONMENTAL CONDITIONS AND INDUSTRY CHANGES

There have been emerging trends that have impacted our environment and changed various industries. Some of these trends below have led to our most recent recession.

- The banking industry approved many risky home loans
- The housing market was overvalued

- Various businesses and families reported low cash reserves or savings while relying heavily on credit to fund daily living and operations
- Millions of Americans were in debt, and more than 14 million were without jobs
- Banks, insurance companies, and other business closings; GM and Chrysler bankruptcies; and government bailouts
- Health care cost continued to escalate during a period where more than 46 million Americans are uninsured and 130 million people have chronic diseases

Turbulent times were prevalent in the American home environment; in 2009 real estate experienced its worst year since the early 1990s. The value of houses significantly dropped 15–20 percent, foreclosures occurred at record levels, and multiple banks were without money to loan, resulting in historical bank closures. Regardless of the industry, an economic recession or health crisis can have an unfavorable outcome for many Americans.

CHAPTER THREE

TURBULENCE OF LIFE

"Remember each day we awake is a blessing and tomorrow is not promised. Live every day like it is your last." —Michael S. Lawson

On May 17, 2009, I received a telephone call stating my forty-six-year-old brother, Gerald Lawson, was in the intensive care unit at a local community hospital near his home. Throughout his life he was never hospitalized. As I urgently traveled to the hospital, I was puzzled about what could be the cause of his admission into the ICU. Once I arrived I was relieved to see him conscious, talkative, and in relatively good condition. After discussions with him and his wife, I learned that he was dehydrated with elevated blood sugar levels related to his diabetes.

The physician was not available, however the nurse stated that he was stable and that they wanted to get him hydrated and lower his blood sugar levels. I was happy to see that his condition did not appear to be life threatening, and we enjoyed watching a Lakers playoff basketball game. I eventually went home that evening relieved, knowing he would be transferring to the hospital nursing floor and would eventually go home sometime within the week.

The next evening I called Gerald around six or seven to check on him. He answered the phone and stated he was feeling better and would be transferring from the ICU to the nursing floor. I was pleased to hear the good news. During our call, my brother told me he would call me back because the doctors were coming into his room. We did not talk the remainder of the evening, but that was okay because I figured he should get some rest.

The next morning during my scheduled work day, I attended the senior executive leadership team meeting at the Cleveland Clinic. During my route to the meeting, I ran into one of Gerald's best friends, George. I gave George the good news about Gerald's condition predicated on my discussion with Gerald the prior evening. Five minutes after my executive meeting that morning, I received a call from my cousin William stating that Gerald had suddenly passed away. My heart was pounding and I was stunned, shocked, and lost for words. Turbulence began at that moment for me as I exited my place of employment to visit my brother. These difficult times occurred in Gerald's remaining days of life—and began in mine due to his shocking death. I rushed to the hospital, and when I arrived in the building, my heart rate began to increase, and I had a nervous feeling as I approached his room. I walked in and saw him lying in the bed with his eyes closed. He looked like he was pleasantly resting.

I sat next to him, held his hand, and looked directly at his face; I then accepted he was not breathing and was lifeless. My mind was confused because I was shocked how someone who was so young and was never seriously ill or even hospitalized—someone who was active with his family, was happy, was loving, and was close to me—could suddenly leave this world and never return.

There is a quote written by Jonathan Lear in the book *Aristotle: The Desire to Understand* that states, "the life of active thinking, the life of active mind, is a life we can live for only a short period of time." Gerald's death reminds me that life is short and can be turbulent; therefore we must all be active enough to love others, strive to make a difference, and live each day like it will be our last.

I learned that he had died of a heart attack due to complications with diabetes keto acidosis. DKA is a life-threatening form of diabetes with a high mortality rate. I did not know he had DKA until the day he died. I also learned Gerald and his wife did not know that DKA episodes could contribute to killing him. The consequences and seriousness of his diagnosis was not explained to him in layman terms by his physician. Knowledge is power if it is obtained and understood in a timely manner.

The reality is that people must become self-empowered consumers, especially when it comes to their health. As Aristotle once said, "a passive mind is perishable." The turbulence of life related to personal health or organizational health can result in the painful loss of loved ones or jobs.

These challenges in life must compel people to develop a vision and execute an action plan to improve public and organizational health. Through the execution process, there will be challenges related to a period of transition and the eventual implementation of the final phase.

CHAPTER FOUR

ADAPTING TO TRANSITION OF CHANGE

"You should keep on learning as long as there is something you do not know." —Seneca, Roman philosopher

To survive a health crisis, overcome personal challenges, or lead an organization into new direction requires the ability to adapt to change. People or organizational team members possessing proven adaptability may have experienced a three-step transition process that includes relinquishing the past, redefining and realigning for the future, and reenergizing to execute new plan.

RELINQUISHING THE PAST

Abandoning outdated strategies, giving up on unrealistic interests, or accepting it is time to move on are decisions that help move the person or organization to the next step in the right direction for a new beginning.

The U.S. government realized that continuing with outdated policies that allow health insurance companies to not cover patients with preexisting conditions was not acceptable. Legislation was signed in 2010 to stop this practice. This historic change will help prepare corporations, the government, and Americans for the realignment of health insurance policies and the upcoming health care reform.

The average American may, as a child, have dreams or interests for many years, such as becoming a doctor, being a professional athlete, or winning the lottery. Financial circumstances may not allow someone to afford medical school; a knee injury might have ended a promising collegiate athlete's career; wasting thousands of dollars annually on lottery tickets is not a logical way to become rich. It is time to relinquish the past related to unrealistic interest and to begin to make changes.

Successful CEOs who are more than sixty years of age and have led their organizations for more than ten years eventually decide to retire and move on to the next chapter in their lives.

For example, Jack Welch of General Electric and Floyd Loop of the Cleveland Clinic led their organizations from the late 1980s to early 2000s before retiring. They retired at the top of their game, producing record-breaking sales and profitability while saving lives and producing products and services that successful satisfy human needs.

The decision to retire at the top of their game from organizations that were part of their lives for more than twenty years was difficult. These decisions required leadership, courage, and vision to allow others to lead the organization into the future. Board decisions to relinquishing the past are tough but necessary decisions of the transition process.

REDEFINE AND REALIGN FOR THE FUTURE

When the past is eliminated, the future can be created through the concepts of re-finement and realignment. They are the main components of the transition process that requires leaders to clarify problem and purpose, establish patterns and structure, and pursue innovation.

CLARIFY PROBLEM AND PURPOSE

There is an old saying that you must go back before you can move forward. Understanding the past can be helpful in understanding the root cause of the problem. For example, problems contributing to the recession included the stock market inflating stock prices and the banking industry approving risky mortgage home loans with high variable rates to home owners with limited or questionable ability to handle turbulent times.

As the stock market declined to 7000, interest rates increased and the economy went into a recession in 2008; savings and investment accounts plummeted, homeowners defaulted on home loans, and banks began closing in record numbers. To eliminate these problems, in 2010 the U.S. government began embarking on new financial regulations for the banking industry and stock market. Clarifying problems can help realign for the future in business and personal life.

If people's unhealthy past contributed to them being excessively overweight or diabetic with high blood pressure, then their doctors will tell them to stop smoking and start exercising, or to replace pork, red meat, and sweets with fish, fruits, and vegetable. The patients' past contributed to their current problem, and it's important they understand root cause of problem and eliminate it with new, good habits.

After the problem is understood, the purpose in the transition process is to realign away from the past and move into a more structured and organized pattern linked to new values, habits, and behaviors that will result in innovation and improved performance for the next step of the process.

REENERGIZE FOR EXECUTION

The next step is the implementation phase of leading organizational or personal change in turbulent times of transition. Transitioning through the change process for the implementation phase cannot be achieved alone. Aligning as a team to achieve a common goal, possessing sincere passion, having technical capabilities and skills, and having an incentive offered to help fuel efforts will help reenergize the team for execution.

A plan is only successful when it is effectively executed. The implementation plan must have quantifiable and observable goals, aligned tactics, qualified and capable teams, realistic timelines, and weekly performance monitoring to ensure accountability.

I recall participating in best-practice methods while executing plans as an executive at the Cleveland Clinic and Ohio Health corporations. These world-class organizations established effective management and decision making structures, recruited the best talent within the industry, and treated associates with great respect to help energize the team.

Both organizations had visionary leadership that anticipated change, prevented crisis, and prepared for the future. They shared a similar mission that focused on serving and improving the health of the customers they served. Their vision, planning, and execution allowed them to efficiently and carefully move through the transition process.

CHAPTER FIVE

HISTORICAL VISIONARY LEADERSHIP IN TURBULENT TIMES

"Be the future you want to see." —Mahatma Gandhi

In turbulent times we all realize that now is the time to recognize the sense of urgency, the need for change, and a vision for the future. Visionary leadership is required to direct the organization or family through the storm of life and to safely land at the desired destination.

Effective leaders understand the current direction of their organization during challenging times. They also realize the need to establish a new direction in order to renew their organization and create a new future.

This chapter illustrates several famous leaders: John D. Rockefeller, Martin Luther King Jr., Ernest Withers, Jack Welch, Abraham Lincoln, Lou Gerstner, Floyd Loop, and John Pope Paul II. These men had a vision to overcome and avoid turbulent times.

JOHN D. ROCKEFELLER (1874–1960)

Mr. Rockefeller was a visionary leader who became the first billionaire and the richest man in America. John was a strategic thinker at a young age and

.earned a great deal from his parents. A quiet boy, he was very good in math and was known to be cautious, patient, and persistent in his thinking and decision making. He admired his father's adventurous personality, business acumen, and love for money.

He adored his mother's bravery and Christian-based faith while raising five children during the challenging times of his childhood. She also taught him the importance of economy, order, and thrift. These lessons helped him and his company during turbulent times.

Rockefeller experienced turbulence at the age of twenty-five when he sought to acquire a loan to expand the business, but his partners, the Clark brothers, refused; they wanted him out of the partnership and requested the business be auctioned off. The Clark brothers were confident they would purchase company at the auction and damage Rockefeller's career.

However young Rockefeller was much smarter and anticipated that his partners would ask him to leave the partnership. He staged the strategy to seek a loan and expand the business to generate their response. He took this action because he already had a new funding partner to help him outbid the Clark brothers and take over the company. He was successful and became the owner of one of the largest oil companies.

After the Civil War, the oil industry became a depressed and overbuilt industry with plunging prices, declining profits, overcapacity of refineries, and ruinous competition. As time progressed, Rockefeller's wealth and career was in jeopardy, but he was trained to always see an opportunity in every turbulent situation or crisis, and therefore he focused on comprehensive solutions related to long-term planning and strategic alliances. His visionary solution was to reduce overcapacity, stabilize pricing, and rationalize the oil industry by doing the following:

- Gain access to capital to create economies of scale
- Build up cash reserves to overcome economic downturns
- Use money to heighten efficiency and eliminate refineries with excess capacity
- Build an expanded oil empire by purchasing many refineries and consolidating
- Develop alliances to address railroads, freight rates, and competition
- Freeze industry size and stymie new entrants

Rockefeller's vision and execution of his plan was successful and allowed Standard Oil to overcome a crisis and demonstrate leading change in turbulent times.

Rockefeller's cautious and strategic leadership style should have been adopted to possibly prevent the British Petroleum oil spill crisis that occurred in 2010.

MARTIN LUTHER KING JR. (1929–1968)
AND ERNEST WITHERS (1920–2007)

Martin Luther King was a great visionary leader that I admired because of his courage demonstrated in difficult times, desire for justice, ability to communicate, and capacity to influence many people into the future. I did not realize how much I had in common with this great leader until I read his 1998 autobiography edited by Claybourne Carson.

For example, I was born in 1964, the legislative recognition year of the civil rights law. Both him and his dad originally had the first name of Michael. My mom and his mother's name were Alberta. Finally, Dr. King had an interest in the healthcare field and we both strongly believe in justice and dedicated our career to improving rights and opportunities for all people including minorities.

Dr. King believed we all should stick together and be united during difficult times. This belief holds true today as we recover as united Americans from a economic recession, begin the health reform journey, and join as a family to overcome health crises.

He was able to anticipate an upcoming problem, formulate a plan, influence millions of Americans towards a common goal and produce an effective solution. He was passionate and believed in the civil rights purpose. His was so compassionate that he sacrificed his life for the cause.

Martin Luther King Jr. had a vision that the United States would be a country with a culture of love, righteousness, and justice that would allow all men and women, including African Americans, to be treated fairly. Ernest Withers shared MLK's vision, marched with him, and experienced major challenges in life that required courage and compelled him to become self-empowered in his career to make a difference in the civil rights movement. There are many articles on Google that tell about the turbulent times of Dr. King and Ernest in the 1960s.

Ernest was a nationally known photographer who marched with Martin Luther King Jr. and played a key role in helping initiate the civil rights movement. Before his death in October 2007, Ernest was able to document throughout his career memorable moments in the turbulent times of the movement. Examples of those moments are published in his book titled *Pictures Tell the Story*.

Ernest Withers marched with Martin Luther King Jr. in 1965 after the death of Mr. James H. Meredith, first African American enrolled into University of Mississippi. They had a vision to build a coalition and develop a national plan to overcome the turbulent times of the civil rights movement. Fifty-three years later in 2009, an African American, Barack Obama was elected as the United States president, and the *New York Times* reported that Attorney General Eric Holder began reshaping the Justice Department's Civil Rights Division to revive civil rights enforcement.

Dr. King once said, "This is no time for apathy or complacency. This is a time for vigorous and positive action." We all have the opportunity to take action, overcome challenges, redefine future direction, and tell our story.

FAMILY AND UNITY

The picture below tells the story of family unity. The picture shows Ernest Withers in the center, my grandmother Rose Washington to Ernest's right and other family members of Ernest.

My grandmother took action and anticipated the future direction of her children and what they may experience in difficult times. She had a vision of her children staying together as a family and living within close proximity. Before she died she purchased four houses for her four children. The houses were on the same street and remain in the family for her grandchildren and their children. The four children were able to control cost and survive the poor economy in the 1990s and during the 2008–2010 financial crisis while never paying a mortgage.

Rose Washington was committed to serving the community throughout her life, even up to her last days before passing away. She fed the hungry every weekend until she was bed ridden and could no longer walk. Her community efforts were recognized by the mayor and the city council. She demonstrated unconditional love to everyone and helped many during difficult times. The picture below shows me and my grandmother together over my mother's home.

Family is our most precious jewel that always must be valued, appreciated, and supported, especially through times of need. Mothers are the most loving family members who are there when you need them the most. My loving mother, Alberta Washington–Miles, experienced turbulent times raising four children. Her determination to work hard and succeed allowed her to overcome life's challenges and successfully raise her children to adulthood.

My dad remarried at a young age to an adorable lady named Carolyn Lawson. Carolyn was employed as manager in the human resource department at General Electric. Carolyn helped me start my ongoing journey into corporate America through summer employment at General Electric. I always admired my parents because I viewed them as leaders of their families as well as their personal lives. This interest in leadership proliferated once I became member of the GE family. I became very interested in business management and therefore began to study the many great leaders of history.

JACK WELCH, (1935 –)
CHIEF EXECUTIVE OFFICER, GENERAL ELECTRIC

Jack Welch anticipated turbulent times and saw the upcoming period of slow growth, increasing competition, and the challenge of improving profits and stock prices as well as leading multiple General Electric businesses. He knew that in order to survive, a business needed to have a sustainable competitive advantage. GE had a competitive advantage in high technology, service, and core products such as lighting and major appliances.

Welch had a vision to become the top-ranked market leader in each business field and sell those businesses who could not achieve his vision. Jack created a sense of urgency that resulted in the selling, closing, or divesting more than one hundred businesses, the development of an innovative product and service research division, and the business acquisition strategy that is still alive today after his retirement and that has existed for more than twenty years.

He achieved his market leadership vision and was also awarded for market value. In 1981 when Jack took over, GE had a market value of $1.6 billion. By 1998 GE's market value reached $250 billion. General Electric became one of the top-ranked companies in American history.

ABRAHAM LINCOLN (1809–1865)

Presidents can experience personal obstacles and have an impact on American history and human life in turbulent times. Abraham Lincoln experienced the turbulent times of personal family tragedies, two senate election bids, the Civil War, and unfair treatment of American citizens.

Abraham Lincoln was born in a log cabin on a dirt farm in Kentucky. His father, Thomas Abraham, witnessed his own father get murdered. This tragedy resulted in unfortunate circumstances for Thomas as a child, resulting in difficult times, a lack of education, and a life as a laboring carpenter. Thomas later married Abraham's mother, Nancy.

Nancy Lincoln was a brilliant woman who was very intelligent and loving. She loved her children and taught young Lincoln to read and spell. They enjoyed reading the Bible. The belief was that Lincoln got his strong will, kindness, and intelligence from his mother. His foundation was built from the experience of hard work, humbleness, difficult times, and poverty that his dad endured.

Before becoming president, Lincoln had to overcome unbearable turbulent times related to poverty and personal family tragedies. Turbulence occurred early in life when Lincoln lost his infant brother and loving mother to fatal ailment when he was only nine years of age. His sister also died during childbirth when Lincoln was nineteen, and his son Willie died in 1861.

Despite Lincoln's family losses, unproductive childhood, inadequate schooling, and meager wages of marginal livelihood, he had courage, a strong desire to learn, a great sense of humor, the ability to tell compelling stories, an exceptional level of intelligence, big dreams, ambitious plans, and the desire to help the unfortunate.

Lincoln loved to read, had a great memory, and became an excellent orator and effective lawyer, which eventually led to an interest in becoming a senator. Despite building a coalition of supporters and voters, Lincoln's first defeat involved him giving in to his opponent and asking his supporters to support the opponent in the best interest of the party. His second loss to become a senator did not deter his political plans. He had developed a strong will to succeed at an early age, driving him to overcome his personal tragedies and political defeats to win the presidency.

As president, Lincoln experienced turbulent times during the Civil War. In order to overcome difficult times, a leader must be engaged to understand the problems and opportunities. His management style was very hands-on; for example, he made rounds at the ground level with the troops, offered direct access to himself in an open-door policy, and directly acquired intelligence. He led by example and expected his generals to emulate his philosophy. General John Fremont was relieved of his duties because he did not follow this management style. Lincoln eventually won the Civil War.

Lincoln had a vision of independence and freedom for all Americans, which eventually resulted in the elimination of slavery and the preservation of the

Union. Lincoln understood the American culture and human nature in those years, and others may have viewed him as contradicting and inconsistent in his values related to slavery, however Lincoln had the ability to make tough decisions, the courage to fight against the odds to save the Union, and the determination to overcome turbulent times and sign the Thirteenth Amendment on February 1, 1865, to end slavery.

LOU GERSTNER, (1942 –)
CHIEF EXECUTIVE OFFICER, INTERNATIONAL BUSINESS MACHINE

Lou Gerstner came to IBM with a vision to create a full-solution, customer-responsive company that would return back to profitability. IBM was a traditional company that had old technology, an alarming rate of declining sales and profit, and a lack of cash. Microsoft and Intel were growing and had captured the new PC and software market while growing IBM needed to restructure and survive.

In order to overcome IBM's turbulent times, Lou had to lead a culture change. Lou stated in his book *Who Says Elephants Can't Dance* that "management does not change culture, management invites the workforce to change the culture." Gerstner identified an intelligent work force, inspired them to believe in themselves and their values, defined the market realities, established goals, designed structures, and created incentives.

Lou achieved his vision. He quickly assessed and recruited his new team, diagnosed the problems, developed a strategy, and returned the focus to the customers. Massive expense reductions were implemented through layoffs, the reengineering of processes and systems, and the elimination of redundancy in operations. Unproductive assets were sold to raise cash. Under Lou's leadership, a global enterprise was established, the brand was revived, and IBM invested in growth markets to help return to profitability.

FLOYD LOOP, MD, (1936-)
CHIEF EXECUTIVE OFFICER, CLEVELAND CLINIC

Floyd Loop was a cardiothoracic surgeon turned CEO of the Cleveland Clinic, one of the top hospitals in America. When Loop took the reins in 1989, the greater Cleveland health system was generating $645 million in net revenue and projected to lose $175 million within 3 years. The Florida facility was hemorrhaging $1 million a month, and the organization needed a vision for the future.

Dr. Loop had a vision of the clinic becoming a profitable, top-ranked, and world-class health care organization, expanding market share and excelling in research, education, and service to the patients. After his first year, Loop turned a negative $30 million cash flow into a positive $30 million. He led a bifurcated initiative to contain cost while amassing market share throughout northeast Ohio. Loop worked closely with board members such as Art Model and the late Al Lerner; both men were owners of the Cleveland Browns. In addition, Loop sought the advice of board member Samuel Miller, chairman of the internationally known real estate corporation Forest City Enterprise.

Under Loop's leadership and with board support, the Cleveland Clinic went from a two-hospital system located in Cleveland and Florida to a fourteen-hospital medical empire comprised of new freestanding clinical institutes, acquired hospitals, and newly constructed regional medical centers and ambulatory facilities in northeast Ohio, Florida, Canada, Las Vegas, and Abu Dhabi. Below is a picture of Loop in the center with Samuel Miller (chairman of Forest City Enterprise) to the left and Michael Lawson (former Cleveland Clinic executive) on the right.

Loop's visionary leadership resulted in the Cleveland Clinic becoming the number-one ranked hospital in heart care; it was also ranked within the top five hospitals in more than sixteen specialties. The organization reported a financial turnaround under Loop's leadership, turning losses into profits and improving revenue from $645 million in 1989 to $3.6 billion in 2004 while sustaining the most important mission: to better serve all patients.

POPE JOHN PAUL II (1920 – 2005)

The entire world knew of the great visionary leadership of Pope John Paul II. He served as the second-longest-serving pope from 1978 to 2005. His leadership changed the course of history in Poland, Eastern Europe, and across the world. During turbulent times he was instrumental in ending communism and improving relations with Judaism and other religions.

He was a renaissance man whose vision included healing the sick, helping the poor, symbolizing love, serving humanity, and loving young people. He knew young people were the future, and through his leadership he had a vision that resulted in the creation of World Youth Day for young people. The pope loved all people and supported all religions and races.

CHAPTER SIX

CULTURE CHANGE

"See yourself and what you see you will become." —Aristotle

UNDERSTANDING CULTURE

I recall a quote that stated, "It is only in the storm, that we truly become sailors and pilots." As the tides may push the ship off course and turbulence rattles the plane from its direct path, the need for adaptability, focus, and change becomes vital.

One thing that is constant in life is change. The economy can go into a recession, growing expenses can erode profit margins, or a new business can enter the market and capture market share from a competitor. No matter the situation, we must be proactive and capitalize on change.

The anticipation for change can help prepare for challenging times that require the need to be innovative and begin the process of modifying one's culture. Culture is a set of values, guidelines, and even policies that reflect behaviors, habits, decisions, and actions taken in business or one's personal life. Now is the time for new ways of thinking and acting in order to survive in life and business.

CULTURAL ASSESSMENTS

In order to overcome problems and succeed in life and business, efforts must be taken to change corporate or personal cultures. Traditions, habits, behaviors, and values can reflect the established culture that may have contributed to root causes of problems. Addressing the primary driver of problems requires a detailed assessment analysis.

During turbulent times a cultural assessment is necessary in order to understand strengths and address weaknesses related to the root causes of problems and subcultures within the overall culture. An assessment or audit can be implemented in the form of interviews or establishing a profile of the current culture.

Interview questions should be developed to identify strengths, weaknesses, habits, patterns of behavior, vulnerabilities, preparation for the future, accountability, profitability, growth, learning environment, cooperation, and resistance. Answers to these questions can improve understanding, strive toward changing the culture, close the performance gaps, and align with the profile.

A corporation or individual profile could include a rating scale ranging from always to sometimes, occasionally, and never. The categories to be rated can include clarity around vision, values, goals, performance expectations, and accountability. Other areas can be alignment with financial management; ability to be change; committed customer service; and focus on health, wellness, and personal leadership.

LEADING CULTURAL CHANGE

Everyone is considered a leader of his or her personal life, family, job, or business. With leadership comes a strong spirit to take on difficult tasks and apply necessary discipline to make tough decisions and create change for the better. Change will require courage. J. Oswald Sanders stated in his book *Spiritual Leadership* that "courage is that quality of mind that enables people to encounter danger and difficulty firmly." J. Oswald, Sanders, Moody Institute publisher, 1994, page 59.

Culture change will require courage, and it must start at the top of the corporation or family so that each member of the team can buy into it. Leaders must create a sense of urgency because time is usually not on their side. In corporate or personal leadership, the message must be clear, compelling, and consistent, combined with immediate action to begin the process.

Other things leaders must do to drive cultural change include demonstrating authenticity and personal values consistent with new culture; proving current culture is a problem; and developing strategy, tactics, and programs that align with the new culture. This method is especially critical in financial management.

COST MANAGEMENT CULTURE

I recall back in the 1980s when I was an unemployed student in college who had access to obtaining several credit cards. I remember opening eight credit cards, incurring twenty-five thousand dollars' worth of debt, and having no source of income to reduce the debt.

As a young adult, I did not realize the unfavorable turbulent impact the high debt, lack of payments, and no income would have on my life. My credit score was in the 500 range, I could not get a loan for a new car, and my ability to purchase a home was low. It took me 10 years to pay off the credit debt and college loans and improve my credit score by more than 740.

Many Americans did not do well financially during a recession in 1930s and 2009, possibly due to prior poor decisions related to high levels of spending, low amounts of savings, low cash reserves and minimal days cash on hand. These cultural ways or poor habits contribute to turbulence and require immediate change.

Change begins by taking a leadership role with oneself, one's family, or one's corporation to be more receptive to adopting a cost-management culture. Controlling and tracking expenses are critical components of the cultural transformation process. Information needs to be collected in order to understand the cost structure and to control expenses.

Activity-based cost systems will help reveal the cost structure, detailed line item expenses, and primary cost drivers. From a personal finance approach, I recall tracking my spending activity for a nine- to twelve-month period within a spread sheet. The expense categories were reported horizontally across the top of the spread sheet, and each daily expense amount was entered vertically on the left side of the spreadsheet. Category totals, averages, and graphs were created to understand cost drivers, structure, and detail activity.

In corporate accounting and finance, activity-based cost measuring helps one understand resource consumption. For example, expensive resource could include cost drivers such as labor hours and units produced such as materials, supplies, and invoices produced. In corporate cost management, the labor line item expense can account for more than 60 percent of total cost and represents a cost management opportunity and a cash outlay review.

In turbulent times an assessment must be undertaken to understand how much cash is spent on each line item expense. Spending must be curtailed, and there must an emphasis on eliminating the following:

- Labor hours
- Entertainment and restaurant expense
- Air travel and hotel
- Credit card expenses
- Shopping for clothing and use of outside vendor services
- Extra inventory and supplies
- Equipment
- Magazine, advertising, and printing expenses
- Additional insurances and maintenance contracts

WELLNESS AND HEALTH MANAGEMENT CULTURE

Difficult economy and poor financial health can unfavorably influence the health of a corporation or individual. It is time to have a shared vision and strategy that produces a future state of long-term health, improved wealth, shared knowledge, and growth. In order to achieve this future state of being, a sense of urgency must be created with immediate interventions to resolve problems aligned with rewards to encourage ongoing desired behaviors.

As a result of these efforts, one should effectively address behaviors that lead to spending time and money on unhealthy habits and behaviors related to excess spending, debt incurred, or disease of the body predicated on toxic food consumption and sedentary lifestyle.

The shared vision can reflect core values that have a direct correlation with guiding behaviors relative to cost-management control, teamwork, information sharing, elevated cash reserves through savings, aerobic exercise, and healthy eating habits. These behaviors can improve the culture and health of an organization or individual.

This new culture is predicated on execution and accountability, which can be the blueprint to a promising future and prevent future financial disasters, economic turmoil, organizational or personal health crisis, family break-ups, or other turbulent challenges.

Once a culture is established, sustainability is likely and long-term health can become reality.

SERVICE CULTURE

Customer satisfaction is the key outcome in establishing a service culture. If customers are satisfied, and organizations or individuals offering a service or product are competitive and innovative, market share will increase or be sustained. In order to satisfy customers no matter the industry or situation, a service excellence culture must be established.

Low satisfaction can result in challenging or turbulent times in marriages, hospitals, businesses, and even personal health. For example, there was a hospital with low physician morale, employees lacking service accountability, an unstable management team, and unhappy patients—all this resulted in patient satisfaction scores in the fiftieth percentile, declining sales volumes, and a need to change leadership.

Senior management made a decision to overcome the hospital's turbulent times by establishing a service excellence culture. There were five key steps that helped establish the service culture: creating a vision, establishing a numerical target, recruiting a new CEO and COO, developing an action plan, and designing a system of accountability.

Senior management created a vision and communicated values that set a framework to support a service culture. They galvanized management and employees to believe they could become exceptional industry leaders in service, and they demonstrated actions and behaviors that reflected putting customer's needs first.

Values of trust, communication, collaboration, and innovation helped ensure customer retention. It was essential that patients could trust their lives were in good hands with physicians and support staff, and so the staff made a commitment to deliver safe and courteous service that resulted in trust and favorable health outcomes.

Constant follow-ups to customers regarding the status of their visit guaranteed a systematic approach to the communication strategy. In addition, taking out the time to sit down with customers and explain service and answer questions helped build relationship and allowed for one-on-one communication.

The need for collaboration and coordination of various departments to provide exceptionally efficient service was of paramount importance. Due to coordinated efforts, teams were created to study processes, policies, industry benchmarks, customer survey results, and employee performance.

Through this process teams collaborated to be innovative and develop new solutions to better communicate and serve patients courteously, reduce steps of delivery of care process steps, decrease patient wait time, enhance the facility, and improve satisfaction scores. The outcomes of these efforts resulted in the following innovative outcomes to help establish a service excellence culture and improved satisfaction scores.

1. Press Ganey patient scores increased from fiftieth to ninety-sixth percentile in six months.
2. The hospital developed a guest service liaison to greet customers and improve way-finding.
3. Hiring policies were modified to recruit based on service standards and values.
4. The hospital implemented free parking, newspapers, concierge services, flowers, and follow-up service calls.
5. Improved staffing ratios increased provider access, appointments, and service.
6. Renovated facilities improved the overall comfort, temperature, ambiance, and appearance.
7. More engaged management and employees were committed to service excellence.
8. The staff held weekly systematic accountability meetings reviewing performance and plans.
9. The hospital Recognized change agents, moved in fence-sitters, and moved out resisters.
10. The company maintained a program of leading change through the transition period.

CHAPTER SEVEN

LEADING CHANGE

"Do not follow where they may lead. Go instead where there is no path and leave a trail."

The United States economy in 2009 was is in a state of crisis. Economists reported we were in a recession. In 2008 the unemployment rate was 7.2 percent, and it exceeded 10 percent in 2009. In 2008 2.6 million people lost their jobs. In 2009 the cumulative number of Americans without jobs exceeded 14 million. As Americans continue to lose their jobs in 2010 after a recession, spending will decrease and loss of health benefits will increase. Health reform can stop the benefit loss. The loss of health benefits can result in an unhealthy America in 10 big ways:

- Uninsured exceeding the record number 46 million and now at 50 million as of 2009
- Declining demand for use of doctor's offices and hospitals
- Increasing use of high cost ERs instead doctor's office and preventive care
- Elevating cost of care due to late stage illnesses and prolonged length of stay
- Declining capital investments due to poor balance sheets and cash flow

- Increasing uncompensated care for hospitals
- Increasing closure of hospitals due to cost of care exceeding revenue
- Increasing health care disparity gap between the insured and uninsured
- Advancing levels of acute and chronic illness due to delayed care
- Increasing probability of co-morbidities and possibly death

As economic times grow ever more into a downturn, an opportunity for change greatly increases. The appointment of a new president has come at the most opportune time to address the health of Americans and the economy. Through the Obama-Biden administration, the release of a stimulus package for job growth and a health care plan for expanding the coverage for all American helps begin this change process.

However in order to change, the following five areas of management must be present for stabilization and future growth to occur: superior strategic structure, presence of mind attack advantage model, strategic financial planning, a renewal of the core, and leading change. There are many stages in a major change process, which are described in *Leading Change* by John Kotter. A few of these include:

- **Establishing a sense of urgency.** Mounting financial losses creates a need for action. All business organizations, including hospitals, are affected by the economic crisis and are examining their competitive markets along with opportunities to reduce cost and become more efficient in order to survive.

- **Creating a guiding coalition.** The alignment of entrepreneurs, physicians, executives, and others, along with the support of board members and employees within the organization, can create a powerful team equipped to lead a major change. Acting as unit to serve customers and restore the enterprise back to financial solvency is critical to the community and signifies team success.

- **Developing a vision and strategy with short- and long-term wins.** To create change, CEOs and the management team are responsible for creating a vision and developing executable plans for achieving that vision. Plans created around renewing core profitable growth services and eliminating non value are duplicative services. Being able to demonstrate growth and cost management are important requirements to generating wins.

- **Communicating change vision and empowering broad actions**. Multiple vehicles such as quarterly leadership forums, weekly website updates, blogs, newsletters, and monthly meetings, can be used to communicate vision. Creating flexibility within team member roles that allow freedom to act and eliminating obstacles, systems, structures, and individuals that impede progress are imperative.

When a crisis occurs and change is required, it is time to consider implementing some of the stages in your change process to ensure the establishment of a superior structure.

CHAPTER EIGHT

SUPERIOR STRUCTURE DESIGN

"First we shape our institutions and afterwards they shape us."
—Winston Churchill

Change cannot be effective without a superior structure that produces good judgment calls. Noel Tichy and Warren Bennis mentioned in their book *Judgment—How Winning Leaders Make Great Calls* that "the primary purpose is to develop useful framework that will help leaders make better judgment."

Framework is predicated on a superior leadership and management structure that can be institutionalized. The structure should include executives trained, educated, and experienced in strategy, tactics, and leadership. Strategic depth and mobility are critical; the team must be inculcated to be mission oriented, fluid, and flexible, in order to adapt to changing conditions and to take advantage of multiple options and ideas.

Establishing a structure within an organization configured for innovation and designed to systematically generate ideas will help manage a crisis in a changing environment. The Cleveland Clinic, a world-class health care system in Cleveland, Ohio, developed enterprise-wide World Class Service idea database that allows employees to go online via the intranet and submit ideas. This system helped engage employees to participate in improving customer experience, reduce cost, enhance operational efficiency, and improve service.

A superior structure must ensure service excellence, quality, and regulation to sustain growth and profitability. Regulation is necessary to ensure a stable system, increase cash reserves, and avoid financial losses. As the banking and investment industry learned, in order to avoid major financial losses and have healthy profitable growth, regulatory and alert systems are essential. Financial and operational systems, in conjunction with IT, must be set up with sensors to detect trends and sense changes that require immediate and proactive management intervention to avoid a crisis.

These systems help control and reduce cost structures, notify management of market share and cash reserve declines, and proactively stop negative run rates and ongoing percent increases in expense growth that exceeds revenue growth.

To avoid mounting financial losses and additional business and hospital closures, U.S. government, entrepreneurs, corporate CEOs, and business executives are reforming their organizations and structures. For example, during a recession many companies experience rapid declines in sales revenue, profit margins, and cash reserves.

This turbulent activity forced the senior management of many companies to implement short-term and long-term strategies to reduce cost and reorganize. The first step of the process is to perform an organizational analysis of business and management structure. The goals are to become nimble, consolidate, and eliminate excess layers.

Companies should simplify structures that are duplicative, redundant, or excessive. The rule of thumb states there should be no more than seven to ten direct reports per executive. Some span of control analyses are expanding to a one-to-fifteen ratio. It typically takes organizations two to three years to reorganize, however in turbulent times, successful companies with superior structured management teams efficiently operate in increments of weeks and right size their organizations within six to eighteen weeks.

In an organizational analysis, reviewing the management structure is a critical first step. Exhibit A displays an organizational chart of an eleven-hospital health care system with at least four layers of management before directors, supervisors, and frontline personnel structures are reviewed. This health system has a chief executive officer overseeing the entire health system, two regional CEOs each responsible for eleven presidents.

Exhibit A.   Former Organizational Structure

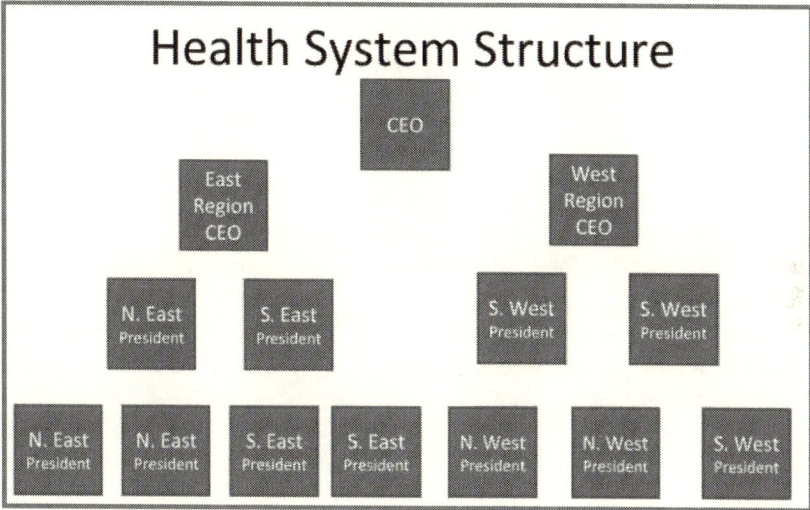

Health System Structure

CEO

East Region CEO

West Region CEO

N. East President

S. East President

S. West President

S. West President

N. East President

N. East President

S. East President

S. East President

N. West President

N. West President

S. West President

Exhibit B.   New Structure

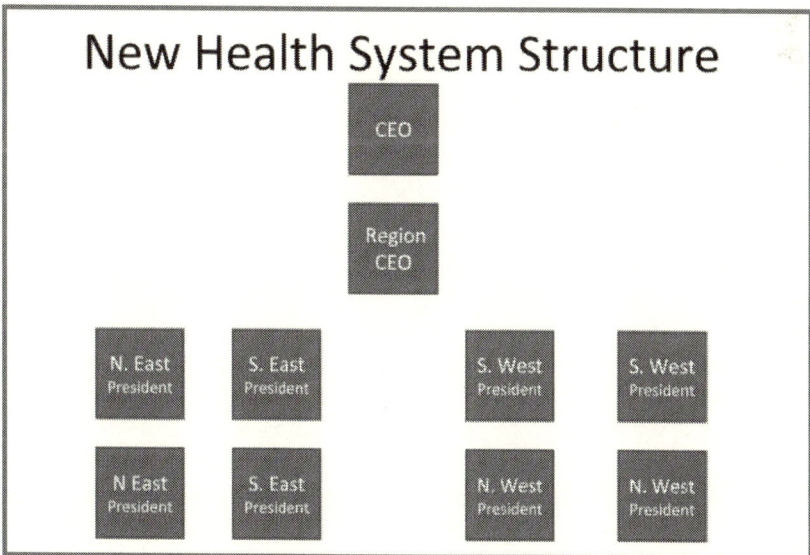

New Health System Structure

CEO

Region CEO

N. East President

S. East President

S. West President

S. West President

N East President

S. East President

N. West President

N. West President

In turbulent times when costs are exceeding revenue and losses are mounting, structures need to be reorganized; the cost should be reduced; and productivity, decision making, and processes should be improved. In the above revised organizational structure, the regional CEO function was consolidated to have all eight presidents reporting to one leader. The regional vice president layer was eliminated, resulting in reduced bureaucracy, elimination of management service duplication, and improved direct communication to hospital. Cost savings in salary and benefit expenses of 3 individuals totaled $1.3 million dollars.

On a much larger scale, a local news paper reported in 2008–09 that Eli Lilly & Company developed and reported a plan to eliminate 5,500 jobs and reorganize into 5 business units. The company will reduce workforce from 40,500 to 35,000 by end of 2011. Cost savings are projected to be $1 billion per year. The reorganization will shift from being organized around functions to a focus on the cancer, diabetes, emerging markets, established markets, and animal health businesses.

Organizational structure change requires multifunctional team effort from senior management to be comprehensive and successful. The reduction of regional layer is only one example; other opportunities exist to further consolidate management functions within the president level by eliminating three positions. This concept can expand to vice president and managers within each organization.

The management team should apply a span of control guidelines that reduce management layers. For example, some corporations have expanded the concept of efficiency by shifting management to direct report ratio from one-to-ten to one-to-fifteen and reducing management layers from the CEO to frontline to six. Management must assess the entire operational structure to streamline, divest, and outsource noncore products and services. This ad hoc approach can apply to individuals, hospitals, banks, the auto industry, and other businesses.

AD HOCRACY STRUCTURE

During turbulent times leaders have learned the importance of an ad hocracy operational structure. Ad hocracy means a combining form of management designed for a specific purpose. The key purpose and concept of ad hocracy structure is to have a multifunctional team working together without borders and traditional bureaucratic structures in order to foresee changing conditions and make timely solution oriented decisions for customers.

This structure has been used in times of crisis to execute turnarounds and establish a stable framework to avoid or effectively manage future difficult times. For example, customers such as patients within a hospital, stock holders of fortune 500 companies, or entrepreneurs of small businesses may find the health of their body, stock value, or cash reserves in a state of deterioration and may require immediate action.

A project-oriented, multidisciplinary team of physicians, executives, or consultants must diagnose the root cause of complex problems, formulate a plan, and execute it to improve the condition, stabilize the deterioration, and develop a recovery plan.

CHAPTER NINE

FINANCIAL SENSE OF URGENCY

"When you arrive at the fork in the road—take it." —Yogi Berra

A sense of urgency is also necessary when corporations are experiencing mounting financial losses and declining market share. Times will get worse before they get better, so establishing a commitment, building a coalition, and executing on a turnaround plan are vital to the survival of the organization. Red flags and symptoms signaling need for a corporate turnaround include:

- Declining revenue and market share
- 30 percent decline in cash flow
- Inability to pay debt and cover payroll
- Increased industry regulations impacting potential decline in revenue
- Unexpected increase in debt equal to or exceeding 20 percent
- More than 70 percent of debt in variable rate
- Eroding profit margin or mounting financial losses
- Consistent declining sales volume

Organizations can be brought back to health through identifying the symptoms and exerting immediate interventions predicated on a turnaround. Trends must be detected early, and new leadership should be inserted to execute change. With the change at the top, a set of fresh critical eyes can detect the red flags and symptoms that reflect emerging trends within the environment and organizations. These trends must be addressed to avoid discontinuities and encourage structural redesign, cash infusion, and cost reductions.

FINANCIAL STRATEGIC PLANNING

Financial planning is an essential component in the financial management process. Planning is necessary in order to establish a direction, improve finances, control expenses, and prevent financial challenges. Improving the financial health of the economy, organization, or individual is critical during turbulent times. To understand the status of your financial health, an operational and financial assessment must be performed proactively.

How can you determine when financial turbulent times are coming? Recent events in the economy related to the 2008–2010 recession and job losses are a few examples. There are warning signs that can serve as indicators of tough times ahead. Paying attention and proactively developing action plans and executing on those plans may help lead you through the changes needed to survive. The following warning sign indicators should signal time for action:

- Consistent trend of declining sales volume and customer base
- Ongoing cost structure increases, high leveraged capital, and revenue declines
- Incremental cost percentage increases exceeding revenue percent increases
- Declining profit margins and cash flows
- Decreases in cash reserves, days cash on hand, and investment balances
- Difficulty meeting debt obligations

To lead change in turbulent times, it is important to analyze financial statements and use ratios compared to benchmarks to determine your vulnerability and liquidity. Seven well-known ratios used include income from operation to sales ratio, current ratio, acid test and cash ratios, days cash on hand, days in accounts receivables, and operating margin. See ratio definitions below.

1. Income from operation to sales ratio must be monitored consistently because a drop in this ratio can mean overall expenses are increasing disproportionately to increases in sales.

2. Current ratio is assets divided by liabilities. This ratio reports the number of times current assets can pay off liabilities. It is preferable to a have two-to-one ratio.

3. Acid test and cash ratios determine how fast debt obligations can be met. Acid test includes cash, marketable securities, and account receivables over liabilities, while cash is the same but excludes receivables. Acid test ratio should be no less than one.

4. Days cash on hand is an important liquidity ratio during turbulent times. Typically you should have 150 days of cash or greater to cover obligation. It is defined as cash and cash equivalents plus other designated funds times 365 days divided into operating expenses minus depreciation expenses.

5. Days in accounts receivables reflect the amount of days it takes to collect uncollected revenue from established accounts. Depending on the industry, exceptional performance is collecting within fifty days or less.

6. Operating margin is total operating revenue minus total expenses divided by total operating revenues. An organization is performing well during turbulent times in the health care industry if their operating margin is greater than 3 percent.

If any of these warning indicators and ratios fall into the high-risk category, most likely turbulent times are on the way. Past proactive financial planning to control spending and acquire assets can be of help because the importance of having assets will be a critical negotiating tool to address debt. During turbulent times problems may occur in meeting debt obligations. Agreements with creditors must be established to avoid defaults, bankruptcies, and poor credit ratings. Debts can be restructured, assets transferred, or stocks exchanged.

The financial health of a corporation or an individual is predicated on their ability to report favorable ratios, pay debt, and sustain a healthy balance sheet. Favorable credit ratings can provide access to capital and create an ability to cover debt obligations. The table below reports credit rating levels for individuals and corporations.

Rating	Individual	Corporation
Excellent	750–840	AAA–A
Good	660–749	BBB–B
Fair	620–659	CCC–C
Poor	340–619	D

The credit agencies reporting personal credit include Experian, TransUnion, and Equifax. Some of the corporate credit and bond agency reporting organizations are Moody and Fitch.

FINANCIAL REGULATIONS

In 2010 the senate and congress agreed to a bill that is expected to be signed to reduce the odds of repeating the financial crisis of 2008 that led to a recession. The bill and upcoming legislation will force the top five to ten banks such as Bank of America, J.P. Morgan Chase, Wells Fargo and Goldman Sachs with assets of $7.5–10.4 trillion or 80 percent of GNP to hold more money in reserves to weather the economic storm. Americans from a personal finance standpoint should apply the same concept in their personal savings accounts.

A network of regulators within new agencies of consumer protection will monitor and police the financial markets that include banks, credit card companies, and mortgage brokers.

Protection will be necessary to prevent mortgage meltdown due to risky loans, credit card variable interest rate hikes, financial firm regulator shopping, and balloon of banking fees.

The financial regulation bill will include the following:

Government	Banks	Consumers	Investors
Regulatory authority to seize troubled firm	Cannot trade own funds	Create consumer protection bureau	Permits SEC authority over broker
Fed oversee community banks	Impose conduct rules of derivatives	Authority to regulate banks/ credit unions	Banks keep 5% of risks on books
Establish 10 member oversight council	Prohibit trust preferred securities	Increase federal deposits to $250,000	Can sue credit rating firms for reckless
Setup liquidation procedure	Limit 3% in hedge and private equity	Ban brokers to steer consumers to risks	Register at SEC as investment advisers
Federal government pick 12 bank presidents	Impose assessment fee on largest firms	States impose strict laws on banks	Shareholders vote on pay and directors
Audit of lending	Cannot bail out funds	State attorney power	Monitor insurance

CHAPTER TEN

RENEWING THE CORE

"All beginnings require that you unlock new doors and remain loyal to your core." – Michael Lawson

The banking and auto industry crisis resulted in a need for loans from the United States government TARP fund to help stop the bleeding of mounting losses related to bad mortgage loans, declines in car sales, elevated cost structures, and other factors.

These crises increased unemployment and the uninsured customer base at hospitals across the United States. Due to these conditions, regulation and change are necessary. As the change process evolves in these industries (including health care), it will be critical to develop strategies to become more efficient and lean. Reviving the organization through the redefinition of core products, services, and capabilities will also be important to the mission and success of the organization.

As the profit pool shrinks, growth rate and competitive advantage erodes, and competitors become a major threat, one should seriously consider the seven steps to redefining the core written in the book *Unstoppable—Finding Hidden Assets to Renew the Core* by Chris Zook.

1. **Develop a point of view on impending turbulence.** Leaders within various industries must demonstrate visionary leadership and determine the speed of change in their markets in order to adapt their organizations to handle turbulent times and manage through the Focus-Expand-Redefine Cycle.

2. **Evaluate the state of the core.** Several diagnostic questions should be asked, such as "What is the current condition of your core customer in terms of profitability, market share, and retention rate?" Other questions related to the state of core differentiation, capabilities, industry profit pool, and ability to adapt to change should be considered.

3. **Identify a set of options.** Due to crisis conditions, an immediate point of departure from current conditions is necessary in order to steer the ship back on course. Strategic options must be established to come to a new point of arrival.

4. **X-ray your organization for hidden assets.** CEOs are always in search for underutilized assets such as team members, products, services, and capabilities provided to customers. These assets offer the opportunity to renew the organization's core.

5. **Refine your set of options.** Once you have identified you're hidden assets, a refinement process is needed with options to ensure the core strategy is developed.

6. **Evaluate options with agreed-upon criteria.** During the evaluation phase, make sure the selected options clearly differentiate your business from the competitor and allow for the ability to restructure and add new capabilities.

7. **Enter the mobilization phase with full force.** Some of the keys to mobilization and execution are readiness planning, consistent communication, relentless follow-through, leading by example, bringing the troops together around a compelling cause, and measuring as well as monitoring performance.

CHAPTER ELEVEN

GROWTH STRATEGY IN A CRISIS

"Never compete with others, only compete with yourself to improve and grow." —Michael S. Lawson

After the core of your business or personal health is renewed, a growth strategy is necessary to move beyond a crisis and get back on the advancement track. The focus of the growth plan can be on the following:

1. Study your health from within and your customers from the outside in.

2. Identify new ways to improve your health and new growth markets for your business.

3. Acquire and build new a personal self-brand, core products, and services for new markets.

4. Develop new distribution channels, alliances, and sales forces to grow the business.

STUDY HEALTH WITHIN AND CUSTOMERS OUTSIDE IN

When a personal health crisis occurs, you must look within to first understand, with the help of your physician, the root cause of your illness in order to prevent it in the future. For example, some people may have developed diabetes and obesity due to lack of exercise and a high intake of foods with high levels of sugar, alcohol, and other carbohydrates. Still others may have developed lung disease due to smoking.

Businesses may wonder why product sales volumes are declining, however they decide it was due to the competitor taking over the market. What the business fails to realize is the changing needs of the customer. The consumers are no longer interested in the same product the business is trying to push on them. Their needs are changing, and competitors are providing product innovations to meet those changing needs. The businesses must stop looking within their existing product lines and start looking outside and into consumer minds to identify their purchasing needs.

NEW WAYS TO IMPROVE HEALTH AND IDENTIFY GROWTH MARKETS

A diabetic, obese, or hypertensive patient is recommended to change their habits by beginning a new exercise program; shifting from an animal-based diet to a plant-based diet; and substituting bad habits like smoking or hanging out in bars with good habits such as eating fruit, drinking eight glasses of water, and spending more time with family. These new methods can improve your health and prolong your life.

Sources of growth come from the needs of the customers, adjacent markets, and segments of the markets that are growing. Defining a new segment of the market is identifying a new consumer need. For example, IBM led the mainframe computer market, but Microsoft and others created a new segment of the computer market with the creation of the desktop, laptop, notebook, and iPad personal computers.

In addition, the cell phone communication market segment was expanded from a simple talking on the phone to texting, searching the Internet, taking pictures, and listening to and downloading music. Even Nike identified new segmented shoe markets: running, tennis, and shoes for NBA players.

NEW BRAND, PRODUCTS, AND SERVICES FOR NEW MARKETS

When people lose weight or overcome a serious, life-threatening illness, others notice the transformation. These changes can help serve as brand activators to support the new self. The new personal brand creates a new image and spiritual awakening that can attract a new life, friends, life mate, and other opportunities.

Acquiring or developing new products and services are other ways to offer innovations to new markets. General Electric and Catholic Health Systems are examples of different companies who grew through acquiring other businesses and hospitals in new markets. These companies also grew organically through research and development, population growth, and satisfying consumer needs. Their brands and companies are strong and positioned well across the nation in various cities. The various site locations, sales staff, physicians, and strategic partners serve as the distribution channels, sales force, and alliances to help grow the business.

Despite turbulent times, companies such as Paycom and the biotech industry have demonstrated growth. These companies have identified growing markets and met the changing needs of consumers. Paycom is a private young Internet payroll company that processes payrolls for companies in the fifty states. According to the Kaufman Foundation study, the fastest growing young companies created 10 percent of the United States' new jobs.

New Jersey biotech companies grew from 238 in 2008 to over 300 in 2009. Growth has been due to the life science industry and the strong, supporting infrastructure from economic incentive programs from the government. Other states with fast growing businesses are California, Texas, New York, Florida, Virginia, Washington DC, and Puerto Rico.

Regardless of the company, a successful formula for growth includes offering value to the customer predicated on need and delivering faster than or before the competition. The key is to enter the emerging market with efficiency and speed, offering an attractive product or service at a competitive price. In turbulent times low-price business acquisitions and takeovers can also be a growth opportunity due to companies needing capital to pay off debt.

CHAPTER TWELVE

PREPARING FOR HEALTH CARE REFORM

"Common wisdom suggests every crisis presents opportunities."
—Scott D. Anthony

Turbulent times in human health have existed within our lifetime for millions of Americans because of a lack of access to health insurance. No health insurance has resulted in delayed medical care, advanced stages of disease, and sometimes death. There is no worse turbulent situation in life than health. Leading change in turbulent times to prevent death requires strong leadership, courage, personal commitment, and teamwork.

On March 23, 2010, strong leadership was demonstrated when President Obama signed the Patient Protection and Affordable Care Act into law. Health reform is now a reality due to the teamwork and courage of the Obama administration, Congress, and the American people. This law will allow for more than thirty million Americans to have health insurance for medical care.

The new law will focus on expanding health care coverage, reducing health care costs, and improving the quality of the health care delivery system. Expanding the coverage will be predicated on a requirement of U.S. citizens obtaining health coverage or pay a tax penalty. There will be a phased-in process for tax penalties based on the following schedule stated in table A below:

Table A. Tax Penalty for No Health Coverage

Amount	Year	Percent of Taxable Income
$95	2014	1.0%
$325	2015	2.0%
$695	2016	2.5%

*The above amounts are flat fees or percent of taxable incomes. After 2016 penalties will be increased based on cost of living adjustments.

In addition to individual tax penalties, insurers of employer-sponsored health plans will receive an excise tax on thresholds exceeding $10,200 individual coverage and $27,500 family coverage. Tanning booths will be taxed 10 percent of the amount paid for indoor service. Many people may also ask where will additional funding come from related to financing health care reform for millions of Americans? Health coverage will be financed through annual fees from multiple sources, several of which are stated below in table B.

Table B. Annual Fees for Financing Health Coverage

Source	Year	Amount
Pharmaceutical	2012–2013	$2.8 billion
	2014–2016	$3.0 billion
	2017	$4.0 billion
	2018	$4.1 billion
	2019–ongoing	$2.8 billion
Health Insurers	2014	$8 billion
	2015–2016	$11.3 billion
	2017	$13.9 billion
	2018	$14.3 billion

Future fees beyond 2018 will be based on the amount of the previous year and the premium growth rate.

Source: www.democraticleader.house.gov/

These sources of funding will help reduce cost of health coverage for Americans and set the tone for hospitals to contribute to reducing excess cost while maintaining quality. A 2008 Dartmouth study reported that in the last two years of life, Medicare spending ranged from $93,842 at UCLA Medical Center to $53,432 at the Mayo Clinic. The Medicare spending average at that time was $85,729, and other top hospitals costs varied but fell below the reported average. For example, John Hopkins Hospital reported $78,666, and the Cleveland Clinic reported $55,333. These figures most likely have increased in 2010.

Medicare is creating other sources for cost-saving opportunities. For example, all hospitals that are organized as accountable care organizations (ACO) and meet quality thresholds can share in cost savings they achieve with Medicare patients. ACOs are accountable for coordinating care, ensuring access to primary care physicians, and reporting quality, demonstrating evidenced-based care and controlling cost for Medicare beneficiaries.

Other sources for cost savings for Medicare and Medicaid patients include the following:

- Payment reform models
- Reduced payments to hospitals for acquired conditions and infections
- Increased drug rebate percentages
- Bundled payments for acute medical, physicians, and outpatient hospital services
- Primary care services provided in-home to reduce and preventable hospitalizations
- A focus on prevention and wellness
- Creation of medical homes and nurse-led clinics

Another method of for hospitals to reduce Medicare cost and improve quality is to reduce readmission rates. The payment system and health care culture must change from encouraging shorter hospitalizations to better managing care after the patient is discharged.

The system must make sure patients have home care, receive a forty-eight-hour follow-up call, have medication management, and can access coordinated, follow-up outpatient care appointments. The *Cleveland Plain Dealer* wrote an article in 2009 recommending what patients and hospitals can do to reduce readmission rates. See below.

PREVENTING READMISSION RATES

What Patients Can Do	What Hospitals Can Do
Don't leave hospital until you understand written discharge instructions	Educate patients regarding diagnosis, explain in layman terms and allow for questions and answers
Ask for home health care if not offered	Schedule appointments for follow-up care and tests
Ask for about follow-up outpatient appointment	Explain test performed, delivery of care process and who is responsible for follow-up
Make sure you have prescriptions and medical equipment (if relevant)	Communicate medication plan and side effects. Discuss intervention steps if problem occurs.
Follow physician orders and contact if needed	Test patient's understanding of discharge plan
Take medications and comply to diet	Implement 2-3 day follow-up discharge call program

Sources: Boston Medical Center, National Patient Safety Foundation, and *Cleveland Plain Dealer*

CHAPTER THIRTEEN

HEALTH CARE CASE STUDIES

The articles I authored in National Association of Access Healthcare Management journal inspired me to share some within this book. Improving access and providing excellent medical care will help save lives in America.

OPERATIONAL EXCELLENCE IN ACCESS MANAGEMENT

As health care reform and legislation becomes law, it is apparent that hospital administration will need help improving access to treat more than thirty million uninsured Americans, finding medical homes for 16 percent of the American population, addressing the 30 percent shortage of primary care physicians, ensuring ongoing patient safety and well-managed medical facilities, and continuing to improve the patient experience.

When a patient chooses a facility for medical services, the first objective in operations management should be to delivery excellent service and satisfy the patient's health need.. Operations are the means by which organizations produce medical services. Excellence in operations requires people, processes, capital, material, and facilities designed around improving access and delivering superior service through the eyes of the customer or patient.

Sometimes it necessary first go back before you can move forward. Going back to the basics to understand the operational drivers of patient satisfaction is necessary before you can move forward to delivery excellence in operations management. Operational excellence in this management chapter will focus on capacity management, patient satisfaction, standards, and governance.

CAPACITY MANAGEMENT

Improving access to care requires management of throughput and patient flow related to physician master schedules, throughput, and staffing.

Physician Master Schedules. The objectives of operations master scheduling are to meet patient demand, maximize capacity, and improve access. For example, each day per week physician A always arrived in the office around 9:00 a.m. and therefore blocked his 8:00–8:30 a.m. time slots. Physician B would use the remaining hours each day per week from 4:00–5:00 p.m. for administrative time; however no administrative outcomes, research papers, or projects were being produced.

Patient demand for first available appointments were greater than normal one week, and both physician-structured schedules prevented timely access to care for patients. Management intervened and opened the appointment slots, creating an opportunity to generate ten to twenty outpatient visits per week (forty to eighty visits per month). Other ways to improve outpatient clinic access are to extend hours into the evening or to open appointment slots on the weekend.

Improving throughput is a strategic priority among hospital executives. As bed capacity problems persist, readmissions rates continue, and more uninsured become insured and seek care, closing the throughput gap becomes critical. A focus on improving the process can be helpful in reducing length of stay, improving discharge process, decreasing LWBS, and ensuring appropriateness of admission. For example, at U.S. hospitals there are online automated systems that report orders written by 10:00 a.m. and discharges by noon by hospital floor, unit, physician, and MSDRG.

Physicians, residents, nurses, and unit secretaries all play a critical role within the discharge process to ensure appropriate orders are written and put into the system. Attending physicians, residents, and others are notified by case managers when delays occur in the key related processes. If problems persist, physician champions, physician chairmen, or administrators are contacted. Other best practices include the following:

1. Physicians with best outcomes share methods at staff meetings and grand rounds.

2. Administrative space is converted into a dedicated discharge holding area, improving flow.

3. The hospital creates a disease management course enrollment to reduce readmission rates.

4. Tests are ordered on an outpatient basis instead of inpatient to reduce length of stay.

5. The staff implements follow-up appointments in nurse clinics and diabetes education.

6. ED and inpatient bed management tracking systems are used to improve patient flow.

7. The hospital uses observation units, Inner-qual, and Milliman and Robert criteria to reduce inappropriate admissions.

Staffing. The delivery of systems within emergency rooms and outpatient clinics has been known to produce outcomes resulting in waiting delays for patients. The practice of adaptive leadership can help solve these operation related problems by using the "on the balcony and into the field" approach to problem solving.

Leaders must get out of their offices and onto the balcony to get a vision of the process. They then should go into the field with the frontline staff and patients to obtain ground-level intelligence to better understand problems and generate solutions.

As executives made their rounds, they witnessed long lines and waiting delays in the ER and outpatient cancer clinics. During the investigation process, a time study was performed that revealed high-volume peak periods in the ER. In addition, between 1:00 to 2:00 p.m. in the cancer clinic, patients were waiting more than thirty minutes to either be triaged by an ER nurse or to be taken to a room by an oncology nurse for assessment. These delays were creating patient complaints, increasing ER LWBS, losing revenue, and frustrating the staff.

The root cause of the ER delays was due to inadequate RN staffing during peak periods, as well as a lack of management interventions. There was only one triage nurse within a two-station triage area. To solve the problems, the nursing team was directed to brainstorm and produce cost-effective solutions.

Qualified nurses assigned to administrative tasks were pulled to staff up during peak periods to assist in the triage process.

The cancer clinic root causes revealed multiple physicians scheduling a higher volume of appointments near the same times, which exceeded bed capacity availability and inadequate nurse-to-patient staffing ratios. Master schedules were modified, resulting in appointments being spread out throughout the day to reduce the bubble and improve throughput. Multiple nursing intake pod systems were established to manage high-volume periods.

The outcomes of both cases resulted in reduction of patient complaints, decreases from forty-five minutes to fifteen minutes in cancer clinic waiting time, more than a 20 percent reduction in ER LWBS, increased outpatient visit volumes, and increased patient satisfaction and physician morale.

Legislation was recently signed to provide coverage for the thirty-two million uninsured Americans. One of the major challenges hospitals face is a lack of physician capacity. There is a 30 percent shortage of primary care physicians. These physicians are needed to serve the thirty-two to forty-six million Americans who may become insured. The government will need to develop innovative ways of addressing this problem. Listed below are a few ideas:

- Higher salaries for primary care and family practice physicians
- Higher reimbursement for primary care, prevention, and wellness
- Use of nurse practitioners and physician assistants
- Flexible work schedules for primary care physicians who are mothers
- Introduction of primary specialty to students starting in elementary and high school

Patient Satisfaction. Improving the patients' experiences during their visits is the objective of hospitals. The patient experience is centered around some key drivers of patient satisfaction that include provider-to-patient communication, education, pain management, cleanliness of rooms, and timeliness of service. The delivery of care process must be designed to address the key satisfaction drivers.

Provider-to-patient communication and education must be designed to deliver compassionate communication that includes greeting patient with a handshake, eye contact, a smile, and a gentle touch on the shoulder. Diagnosis, the treatment plan, and each stage of the delivery of care process must be explained, demonstrating concern. It is also important to provided periodic updates regarding status of visit. If it can be done at restaurants, patients deserve the service relative to their health.

Many patients complain about their pain, lack of timely response to call button, or a dirty room. Systems should be put in place ensure appropriate nurse-to-patient ratios, compliance with pain management protocols, accountability management with environmental service, and nursing management to prevent these problems.

Several hospitals are implementing systems such as rapid-response teams, family empowerment procedures with direct access to management, and ED response teams if call button requests on the floors or in the ICU are not handled in a timely manner. It creates a culture of accountability across all teams. An office of patient experience was created at several hospitals with a physician and nurse co-leadership. Patient experience councils were established at each community hospital within the health system. Each council was responsible for identifying and meeting satisfaction drivers.

Another initiative to improve patient satisfaction involves the executive team creating a sense of urgency by mandating action plans that are reviewed weekly; underperforming departments are summoned to present explanations and solutions until outcomes improve. Other tactics that help are having clinical management teams rounding on a daily basis to engage employees, developing key must haves, communicating with patients, and acting as a unit to solve problems and recognize achievements.

Findings are electronically reported online in the rounding log and sent to senior management. Problems must be addressed and resolved within the established timeframe. Patients in the hospital or clinic are also provided daily comment cards provide feedback.

Each manager is responsible for collecting cards, resolving any issues, and recognizing employees for their great service to the patients. Finally, the patient callback program staff should contact discharged patients, get feedback, and generate a report to management.

STANDARDS AND GOVERNANCE

Operational excellence requires management and hospital employees to comply with established standards and governance. In order to remained accredited, health care organization must follow guidelines established by CMS, Joint Commission, and the States Department of Health. Surveyors and auditors will use patient tracers, life safety, and NFPA guidelines to ensure the safety of patients. In state operation manuals, there are regulations and interpretative guidelines for hospitals to follow. These guidelines are predicated on the conditions of participation.

Each director and manager must have a book of evidence that contains policies, procedures, and supporting documentation predicated on each standard. There are seventy-four standards within the fifteen conditions of participation listed below:

1. Compliance with Federal, State, and Local Laws
2. Governing Body
3. Quality Assessment and Performance Improvement
4. Patient's Rights
5. Staffing and Delivery of Care
6. Medical Staff
7. Medical Records
8. Nursing Services
9. Pharmaceutical Services
10. Radiologic Services
11. Surgical Services
12. Nuclear Medicine Service
13. Outpatient Services
14. Respiratory Services
15. Rehabilitation Services

In conclusion, a commitment to improving capacity management, patient satisfaction and standards and governance can contribute to achieving operational excellence. The outcomes will improve access to care and enhance the patient experience.

HEALTH EXECUTIVE TURNAROUND

The Cleveland Clinic is one of the leading health care institutions in the industry. It is well-known for its world renown physicians, World News Report ranking, acute multispecialty care, and well-managed clinical operations. This not-for-profit institution is reasonably large, with over 37,000 employees. It was reorganized into a multi-institute divisional hospital organization comprised of multiple departments functioning as a private practice model within a large system.

Each division structure is comprised of multiple revenue-generating departments. The freestanding clinical buildings, along with the divisions, serve as mini organizations within the large system. Executives responsible for these organizations have major operational and fiscal responsibilities. The intent is to demonstrate how an executive helped grow and turn around various areas of the health care operations.

I.   REVENUE TURNAROUND

The hospital and clinic organizations in the 1990s and up to 2006 were hemorrhaging cash and experiencing a financial loss in key clinical areas across the institution. The financial losses were complex and linked to several variables such as (1) a need for new management, (2) billing and coding challenges, (3) soaring cost consistently exceeding annual expense budgets, and (4) capacity constraints limiting volume growth.

MANAGEMENT

Due to the mounting losses and financial problems, I as the new administrator/ VP was hired to help energize a turnaround by providing overall leadership, developing and executing a strategic plan, redesigning processes, integrating services, overseeing hospital activities, improving cash flow, and restoring margins as well as long-term financial viability. I was assigned to many areas throughout my career. This turnaround represented initiatives linked to medical and surgical hospital operations, clinical division service lines, and community hospital operations.

All targeted divisional organizations experienced most, if not all, of the financial challenges stated above. Some notable challenges to point out include clinical departments within the division of medicine organization facing declining hospital admissions and mounting ED margin losses exceeding $1.2 million. The oncology division experienced soaring cost and budget problems that created multimillion-dollar, unfavorable variances for three consecutive years. A new neurosurgery brain institute program was under CEO scrutiny after demonstrating slow revenue growth, and the division of radiology was losing billable revenue due to quality control and billing challenges.

Mr. Lawson reviewed reports, organizational structure, and meeting minutes, and he participated in a series of meetings with stakeholders such as the CEO, the board of trustees, physicians, nurses, management, patients, employees, community residents, local ministers, business leaders, and local, state and federal government officials. These reports and meetings helped diagnose root causes of problems, identify solutions, and develop turnaround growth plans.

The physician leadership, administration, and I worked closely together to apply a management model and to develop objectives, action plans, performance metrics and benchmarks, contingency plans, funding, and a new team. Structures were reorganized, resulting in consolidation, elimination, and recruitment of new management and support personnel. Once the plan was approved and the team was in place, Lawson executed an aggressive communication plan to establish communication channels, educate employees and stakeholders, and gain commitment regarding action plan.

BILLING AND CODING

The assessment phase showed declining cash flow related to poor collection of accounts receivables, inefficient charge posting, mounting held claims, and billing denials; these were also linked to inadequate clinical documentation, incorrect coding, and registration errors.

The amount of days in account receivables averaged over one hundred days in medicine and nearly forty-five days in oncology. In addition to poor collections, there were three consecutive years in which over 90 percent of posted charges unfavorably exceeded the four-day target limit. To amplify the problems, coding errors increased held claims to six hundred thousand dollars annually, front desk personnel selected incorrect insurance when registering patients, and physicians inadequately documented their clinical services (resulting in billing denials, under coding, lower fees billed, and inaccurate reporting of case mix).

The following actions below helped turn around the financial performance of the organizations:

- New management and staffing was hired to aggressively call on accounts. Supporting documentation was provided with claims. Delinquent claims were sent to the collection office in a timely manner. There was a 20 percent improvement in net days in account receivable within one year.

- Time studies were performed, and work flow and processes were reviewed. Clerical duties were eliminated from the coding team and reassigned to a clerk. Additional training was provided to coders, and new performance targets were established. As a result modifiers were applied to eliminate held claims, and the four-day charge posting target of 10 percent decreased from 96 percent to an impressive 3 percent.

- Chart audits were performed. Physicians were given monthly reports on their case mix volume and documentation. They received index cards on documentation guidelines. Smart forms were created for doctors to complete. Physicians were encouraged to provide complete documentation of history and physical exam, time spent with patients, reviewing reports and records, interpretation of labs, and discussion with another provider. These changes improved revenue by $1.9 million, increased level 5 coding from 18 percent to 25 percent, and boosted critical care coding from 0.15 percent to 4 percent of total visits.

- Front desk personnel were trained on the new Epic system. The correct primary and secondary insurances were selected and registration denials were below the 5 percent target. A new denial database was also implemented. New EMR was implemented, and physician compliance was monitored and improved.

- Fee structures were compared to market rates and appropriately increased.

- Revenue also increased due to compliance programs, improved access to care, and increased volume of patients.

II. COST REDUCTION TURNAROUND

The hospital profit margins in health care continued to decrease. There are several factors that contribute to this decline. Hospitals knew net collections as a percent of reimbursement were going down year by year. Salaries for employees and agency expense usually increased annually. The need for innovation and capital was vital for organizations to provide state-of-the-art care and sustain their competitive advantage. Unfortunately the cost of technology and pharmaceuticals continued to increase.

The above factors led to the obvious fact that expenses needed to be controlled. The assessment phase reported expenses exceeding budget expectations by $261,440 in 1999, $646,643 in 2000, and $982,680 in 2001. These findings revealed that administrators were not practicing effective cost management. Below are the following actions taken to build a cost-management culture and restore expenses back to expectations.

- Some management positions were eliminated, and other manager's responsibilities were increased.
- Cost management became an agenda item in every management meeting.
- Agency expense and overtime was reduced compared to the previous year.
- Transcription and maintenance contracts were renegotiated to a lower rate.
- Open positions remained unfilled unless totally necessary.
- Medical supply contracts were renegotiated due to changes in physician practices.
- Nonmedical supply expenses were reduced due to inventory management.
- Departments consolidated services and shared FTE resources, eliminating labor hours.
- New travel policies were developed, decreasing expense limits and over travel cost.
- Services and flex budgeting were integrated, and productivity was managed to metric targets.

The initiatives decreased expenses six consecutive years from 2002 to 2007. The total expenses were reduced by more than four million dollars.

III. VOLUME GROWTH TURNAROUND

One of Mr. Lawson's assignments was to help the clinic better serve community-wide markets by improving relationships with the community and providing access to care. The emergency department was founded in the 1940s, and up until 1994 the facility only had eight beds for patients. The facility was located in a hidden location on East 90th street next to a garbage disposal. Community perceptions of access to care were unfavorable.

In 1993 annual visits were approximately 13,425, and margins as well as net income reported significant financial losses. The leadership of Floyd Loop, Sam Miller, and members of board of governors and trustees made a commitment to build a new forty-bed emergency medicine center, a fourteen-bed access center facility, and surgery suites.

This new team developed a strategic plan and increased the physician staff from six to twenty. Support staff was hired to fulfill the mission of the clinic to provide better care to the sick. Marketing, community outreach, and operational plans were important parts of the strategic plan. Policies, clinical pathways, standard operating procedures, and multidisciplinary teams were developed to deliver efficient service and accommodate increasing volume.

After the first year of opening the new facility, visits increased by 66 percent and showed continued growth until it reach near capacity (96 percent) in 1997. Processes were reengineered, and physician productivity improved in 1998 to achieve a 10 percent volume increase. The following actions below were taken to increase bed capacity and continue 37 percent growth from 1999 to 2004. The overall growth since 1993 to 2004 was 317 percent.

- An ED tracking system was purchased to collect data and further improve processes and productivity.
- Offices were converted to clinical space for four additional beds.
- The hospital reconfigured some larger one-patient exam rooms to accommodate two patients while sustaining privacy.
- I negotiated with internal medicine to use their fourteen exam rooms after 5:00 p.m.
- Established an agreement with access center to acquire their fourteen beds and relocate their department.
- Conference rooms and management offices were converted to exam rooms.
- Triage process and staffing was modified to accommodate peak periods.
- Bedside registration and preregistrations initiatives were implemented to improve throughput.

The ED was transformed from an unprofitable operation providing unacceptable access and care to a growing, profitable center of excellence with highly trained medical staff offering high quality care.

Another volume-enhancement assignment was linked to the oncology division. Mr. Lawson received this assignment from CEO in November of 2001. The other objectives were to help increase profitability (stated earlier in the report), improve operational indicators, integrate services, develop community outreach programs, and improve World News Report ranking. The achievement of these objectives helped increase volume. I led the following actions and the graph below show ongoing improvement and growth.

- Reassigned personnel, and enforced HR policies to improve management, reduce cost, and create service oriented culture.
- Formal management team and structure were established to improve communication and create unity.
- Established initiative to improve access by monitoring and reducing appointment cancellations, filling unused appointment slots, expanding work hours, and developing new multidisciplinary clinics.
- Conference rooms were converted to clinical space and additional treatment areas.
- A neurosurgery program was acquired.
- In 2002 & 2003, I met with the CEO and the chief of staff to discuss the acquisition of the medical oncology program.
- Medical services were expanded to community hospitals and family health centers.
- Recommendations were submitted to CEO on how to improve rankings research and earn National Cancer Institute (NCI) designation.
- Educated and energized management team, improving 83 percent of operational indicators through action plans and follow-up.
- The World News Report ranking improved 53 percent from 30 in 2004 to 14 in 2005, primarily due to NCI designation.

HOSPITAL ADMISSION GROWTH AND TURNAROUND

Due to increased bed capacity, improved service delivery processes, and multidisciplinary team collaboration, hospital admissions increased annually until 2002. That year admissions dropped due to policy changes related to one-day length-of-stay hospital admissions. The belief was that some one-day admits resulted in zero payments. Due to this belief, constraints were placed on admissions, and volume and revenue declined.

One day admits were tracked before and after the policy change. Data was submitted showing revenue losses. In addition, other reports showed one-day admits were being paid. and therefore the policy was modified, certain admit privileges were restored, admit categories were changed, volume increased 8 percent, and net income increased by approximately one million dollars in 2003. The 2004 reported hospital admissions accounted for approximately twelve million dollars in net income.

IMPROVING ACCESS TO HEALTH CARE

As the U.S. population exceeds 288 million, the minority population advances to more than 100.6 million, the uninsured reaches nearly 50 million, and chronic diseases and health disparities becomes a major health challenge, the need for improved access to health care and universal health insurance becomes paramount.

To compound the health care access problem, there is a national trend where companies who traditionally provided employer-sponsored health insurance are reducing coverage, shifting the expense to employees, or eliminating coverage altogether. These decisions are predicated on continuous growth in health care expenditures.

Some of these proliferating expenditures are correlated to the care of the elderly; sixteen million underinsured, low-income patients; and chronic illnesses. For example, in 2006 health care expenditures were projected to exceed two trillion dollars, with the elderly and low-income Medicare and Medicaid programs accounting for greater than four billion dollars. Chronic illness is more common in the elderly and poor. Nearly 50 percent of Americans have a chronic condition, and in the next fifteen to twenty years, chronic illness is projected to consume 80 percent of the nation's health care spending.

There is an opportunity to redesign organizational structures and systems to provide more value, greater quality of care, and improved access as well as health outcomes for patients.

A reformed health care system is now law and will require a universal team effort from a special community of organizations such as the U.S. government, insurance companies, pharmaceutical companies, health care-related businesses, health care organizations, physicians, and patients. The above team can be called a formal network.

The formal network will enable teams to work together to stimulate interactions that will mobilize knowledge and talent to address focused topics. The network is designed to have a mutual interest for solutions to focused topics and avoid thick silo walls and matrix structures that delay the implementation process.

The task of this network would be to bring together a community of organizations to do collaborative work related to the creation and sharing of best-practice information designed to do the following:

- Execute a universal health care coverage plan
- Create care management programs to prevent and treat chronic disease
- Establish formal network partnerships and programs to improve access to care
- Design systems and processes to reduce health care cost and improve delivery of service

U.S. hospitals are committed to making their contribution to establishing a formal network to improve access to health care, help eliminate health care disparities, develop chronic disease care management programs, establish strategic partnerships, and design systems that provide integrated as well as coordinated care.

For example, Huron Hospital in Cleveland, Ohio, helped improve access to health care through implementation of their access plan related to four components: access to providers, beds, a new care management program, and health coverage and information.

PROVIDERS AND BEDS

To improve access to physicians and specialty care, Huron Hospital hired and promoted several physicians in specialties such as primary care, endocrinology/diabetes, urology, cancer, geriatrics, cardiology, and pediatrics in 2006 and 2007. In addition, more than twenty nurses were recruited nationally and internationally to support physicians and provide medical care.

Child care, women's health, cancer, diabetes, and minority health are growing concerns within Huron Hospital's service area. Because of this, Huron improved its bed access by relocating its obstetrics and women's center to improve bed capacity more than 150 percent.

A new community health center will be established in 2011–2012 and it will provide clinic beds, outreach, and navigation programs for patients with heart disease, kidney disease, stroke, and diabetes. The program's focus is on reducing health disparity and chronic disease through education and clinical intervention. Additional bed capacity was created for the development of a women's health and men's clinic to address cancer and other diseases. Finally, the cancer center was provided an additional physician to expand hours and days of service.

CHRONIC DISEASE CARE MANAGEMENT PROGRAM

The chronic diseases of focus at Huron Hospital are diabetes, heart and vascular disease, kidney disease, and cancer. I was the vice president responsible for chronic care services and strategic hospital operation initiatives at Huron Hospital and the Cleveland Clinic.

More than 55 percent of Huron's patients have diabetes, and Huron is known for their nationally renowned Lennon Diabetes Center. The center is recognized by the American Diabetes Association as meeting national standards for diabetes self-management education.

Outpatient visits have grown nearly 100 percent in the last five years. Individual education sessions increased by 28 percent from 2005 to 2006. Patients who receive education and treatment have decreased lengths of stay (one day or less), readmission rates (29 percent), and amputation rates (44 percent). These outcomes help reduce overall cost of health care.

In 2007 Huron Hospital created a chronic care interventional center that provides integrated and coordinated care along with community outreach services to patients with kidney disease, heart disease, hypertension, diabetes, and cancer. The center is a clinic that is nurse led with support from physicians, and it provides a kidney disease clinic, heart failure clinic, anticoagulation clinic, and diabetes education services.

The staff is integrated to provide cross coverage and collaborative services as a team to ensure coordinated care and appointments. Other services within the center include a resource and education center; community outreach health talks; and cancer, diabetes, and high blood pressure screenings. The objective is to promote disease prevention and interventional care and to reduce health care disparities.

The final program Huron Hospital recently established was the vascular access program for patients needing venous access for dialysis. The majority of Huron patients are diabetic. Some patients have heart or vascular disease as well as kidney failure. When the kidneys can no longer clean the blood, dialysis may be required. The vascular access program focuses on providing 24/7 access to the community for appointments and vascular surgical services.

There are three types of access sites. The first is the fistula, which is made by joining the artery and vein under the skin in the arm. The second is the graft, made by connecting an artery and vein in the arm with plastic tube. The third is the catheter, which is inserted into a vein in the neck or below the collarbone. The vascular access program is lead by the vascular surgery chairman. Additional surgeons are being trained and recruited to expand the program.

HEALTH INFORMATION AND COVERAGE FOR CARE

Forming strategic partnerships with the community, government officials, insurance companies, and other health care organizations are part of Huron Hospital's strategic plan to establish formal networks, share information, and provide health care coverage.

Health information is shared on a monthly basis throughout the community on the treatment and prevention of cancer, diabetes, and heart disease. Huron also provides applications for patients to determine whether they are eligible for government-funded programs (such as Medicaid) or charity care. Finally, Huron's EMR, MyChart, and Internet-based systems provides patients with access to some of their medical information.

In 2006–2010 Huron showed its commitment to the community by providing over forty-five million dollars in charity care and by serving minorities and the uninsured. There are many other hospitals across the United States that support the poor and deserved to be recognized for their commitment.

To further its commitment, these hospitals partner with the free clinics and other community health organizations to ensure that uninsured patients have additional options to access care. These partnerships are shared with community residents and organizations during outreach efforts.

Providing low-income, elderly patients with access to affordable health care insurance helps eliminate health care disparity and provide value. Huron and others are establishing partnerships with several insurance companies to increase enrollment into affordable Medicare and special chronic disease plans.

The partnership involves the insurance companies and hospitals developing joint outreach initiatives to educate and enroll people in the surrounding communities that the hospitals serve.

CONCLUSION

The increases in U.S. population, the uninsured, and the cases of chronic illnesses along rising health care spending signals a national need for improved access to health care and universal health insurance. If the system is not fixed, costs will continue to escalate, and American chronic disease mortality rates will increase.

Establishing formal networks, redesigning organizations, and reforming health care system are necessary steps to address this problem. Each organization within the formal network has their part in the overall plan.

Hospitals who can improve delivery systems; reduce cost; create new programs; and improve access to providers, beds, and health prevention and treatment information will make important contributions to solving this problem.

Improving access to health care and establishing universal health insurance will require legislation, innovation, and collaboration. The initiative will be a process that takes time; however through strategic partnerships, formal networks, and program development, access and health care coverage will be achieved.

The Obama administration and Congress were successful in bringing historic health care reform to reality. I believe the new legislation is really health insurance reform because many details of the law address insurance coverage. For example, Table 1 below indicates some of the following changes that will go into effect now and the next four to five years.

Table 1 HEALTH CARE REFORM LEGISLATION

YEAR	CHANGE
2010	Pre-existing conditions covered
2010	Cap on benefits over 1 year or life
2010	Small business tax credit for health insurance
2014	Americans earning $200,000 or more will be taxed
2014	Preventive care is free

2014	Adult pre-existing conditions covered
2014	Must have insurance or pay fine:
	$95	1% of income
	$325	2% of income
	$695	2.5% of income
2017–2020	5–10% covered by state (income 133% poverty level)

Source: CNN News

IMPROVING ACCESS TO CARE THROUGH STRATEGIC INTEGRATION

In health care the strategic area of focus is the patient. The hospital strategic planning process is designed around the concept of "the patient comes first," and all decisions will have a direct link to the patient. Americans are aging, and eventually everyone will become a patient.

According to the U.S. Census Bureau report, Americans forty-five years of age and over accounted for 30.6 percent of the total population in 2000. By 2007, this same age group increased 18.3 percent and accounted for 36.2 percent of the total population. During this same period, there was a 58.8 percent increase in Americans that were eighty-five years of age and over. As Americans get older and become patients, the probability of having comorbidities will increase, and the demand for multi specialty coordinated care for chronic disease patients will proliferate.

More than 130 million people are suffering from chronic diseases. Today, seven of every ten Americans die each year from chronic diseases. Some of the leading chronic diseases include heart disease, cancer, stroke, respiratory disease, diabetes, and kidney disease. These diseases are usually identified by the primary care physician.

Hospitals offering primary and multispecialty care have an opportunity to redesign care delivery systems in order to focus on coordinated chronic care and disease management through an integrated approach, leading to a new paradigm of primary and specialty care.

Access to primary care is vital to optimal health and includes both routine and preventive care. An important measurable indicator to determine if patients have access to care begins with a patient having a "medical home" normally found in a clinic or doctor's office. The medical home helps ensure patients have access to chronic disease management and wellness and preventive care. It is the usual source and central position of quality primary care.

Routine follow-up care of fifty- to twenty minutes within the medical home model usually is not sufficient to provide a variety of services. Therefore the use of a nurse to provide the extended assessment, education, and chronic disease management services is recommended to support the physician.

Patients with a chronic disease usually have comorbidities that require specialized care through a referral from a primary care physician to a specialist. These important, strategic, integrative partnerships that hospitals have with their physicians are vital to the health care of America. The coordinated approach to chronic care can improve access to care and health outcomes by utilizing an integrated model of primary care and multispecialty physicians. The strategic integration model improved access to care with direct correlation to six areas of focus: endocrinology, wound care, nephrology, oncology, urology, and community health.

Community hospitals have been committed to providing health care to urban community markets for more than one hundred years. Community hospitals are developing unique partnerships with large academic hospital systems to help fulfill their missions, provide chronic care medical services, and support physician alignment.

For example, due to increasing demand and limited physician staff, Huron Hospital of Cleveland and Cleveland Clinic improved patients' access to chronic care through joint recruitment and integration of physicians within the areas of focus mentioned earlier. The initiative was put into operation through integrating management services, sharing salaries fifty-fifty, identifying physicians with capacity to treat more patients, establishing interest in urban health care, and agreeing to work at two hospital sites. Vice President Michael Lawson is responsible for the initiatives.

ENDOCRINOLOGY AND WOUND CARE

The goal of the integrated hospital partnership was to improve access to care through use of shared physician medical services across two hospital organizations. For example, an endocrinologist employed at the Cleveland Clinic agreed to become medical director of the Lennon Diabetes Center and a researcher at Huron Hospital.

The addition of this physician allowed Huron to establish a new diabetes clinic and an endocrinology fellowship. Patients now have access to additional doctors and a new clinic.

The American Diabetes Association reported that there are over twenty million people with diabetes. It is ranked as the sixth leading of cause of death and is considered a chronic disease. Diabetes is one of the top diagnosed illnesses at Huron Hospital. One of the goals for diabetes patients is to avoid amputations of lower extremities. The wound care services have been able to reduce amputations by 33 percent over the last five years. A component of this success was correlated to the integration of contracted hyperbaric services through physician medical directorship and oxygen therapy. The hyperbaric chambers have the capability to treat ten patients at one time. Huron was able to improve access to wound care through this integrated partnership.

NEPHROLOGY

According to the Center for Disease Control, nearly 26 million people in the United States have kidney disease, and it is the ninth leading cause of death. A National Hospital Discharge Study from 1980 to 2005 reported kidney disease hospitalization increases from 416,000 to 1.6 million. Advanced kidney disease can lead to end stage renal disease. Incidence of ESRD is influenced by demographics of metropolitan statistical area. Cleveland ESRD population reported rates that exceed one thousand per million.

Huron Hospital is one of three the top local Cleveland market leaders in the treatment of kidney disease. Due to the increase demand for kidney care and vascular access services, Huron Hospital and Cleveland Clinic established a joint partnership to recruit nephrologists. The nephrologists have a part-time role at each hospital and will establish a new nephrology fellowship and transplant clinic at Huron. In 2009 Lawson developed a strategic business planned that included development of a total kidney care program that will include a dialysis center, a kidney clinic, an anemia clinic, a hypertension clinic, and a transplant clinic. The new program will be housed in the new community health center.

ONCOLOGY AND UROLOGY

According to National Center for Health Statistics, Cancer is the second leading cause of death, which accounts for 22.8 percent of total deaths in the

United States. Nearly 560,000 people were projected to die in 2008 of cancer. Cancer mortality rates per 100,000 people within Huron Hospital strategic market areas exceed local, state, and national averages.

To reduce cancer health care disparities and improve access to cancer care, Huron and other hospitals made a commitment to expand community outreach health screenings and education initiatives, adopt patient navigator concept, and recruit additional oncologists. The recruitment initiative was a joint project with academic medical centers and community hospitals.

For example, an additional oncologist can split his time between both hospitals. Huron's Cancer Center expanded its physician office 2 clinic days per week to better serve the patients. The additional oncologist will allow Huron to treat more patients, increase cancer prevention health screenings, and expand chemotherapy services.

Prostate cancer is the second leading cause of death for men. In 2006 Huron partnered with Cleveland Clinic's Urologic Institute to establish a men's health center for improved access to urologic and primary care. The urologist splits his time at both hospitals to provide medical and surgical care along with prostate cancer screenings and education. Administrative and management support are provided by hospital.

COMMUNITY HEALTH

Improving the access to care enhances the health of the community residents. Comprehensive community outreach health screenings and education programs serve as portals into primary care and specialty physician offices. Under Lawson's leadership, Huron partnered with Cleveland Clinic to establish a community health program to reduce health care disparities and improve access to health care. Lawson and a Cleveland Clinic executive and physician allocated 50 percent of their time to develop the program and collaborate with Huron physicians and support staff. Several new programs such as a new resource and education center, chronic disease clinics, social services, health talks, and outreach programs were established.

Huron's community outreach program provided free health screenings to more than 1,153 patients in 2007. Follow-up phone call services were provided to patients with the intent to schedule primary care appointments for patients with abnormal results. According to a Huron health screening study, more than 45 percent of patients had abnormal results, and 20 percent were treated at Huron and remainder at other hospitals.

SUMMARY

The strategic integrations improved access to care to more than three hundred new patients and increased outpatient visits by more than 10 percent in 2007. Success continued in 2008 with inpatient discharges reporting double-digit growth for several specialties.

Other integrations included nursing homes and insurance companies. In an effort to improve the payor mix and increase patient access to extended care, hospitals established partnerships that allowed doctors to become medical directors at nursing homes.

In addition, the hospital and partnering insurance company agreed to add physicians to panels and participate in joint community outreach events to attract new patients. Outcomes resulted in a 5–10 percent increase in inpatient discharges from nursing homes and Medicare in 2008.

Strategic integration of the various clinical specialties allowed a community hospital to:

- Improve access to care for aging chronic disease patients
- Enhance service delivery by reducing patient wait time for physician services
- Avoid increase of expenses through sharing of salaries
- Turn around financial performance from a negative to a positive net income
- Improve community health through health screenings and education
- Initiate physician alignment and a coordinated care process that helped redesign care delivery processes of community hospital and specialty care

TRANSLATING DIABETES STRATEGY INTO ACTION

United States health care trends show a growing public health care concern in chronic disease. Currently chronic disease accounts for 70 percent of total health care cost. One of the chronic diseases of concern is diabetes. Diabetes is the seventh leading cause of death. People with diabetes have a better chance than others of having a stroke, going blind, or losing a leg. Diabetes can also cause cardiovascular disease and kidney failure.

According to a 2007 Center for Disease Control report, the number of Americans with diabetes has grown to twenty-four million people. Eight percent of the U.S. population has diabetes, and according to the CDC study, 25 percent of people are unaware that they have diabetes. Another fifty-seven million people have elevated blood sugar called prediabetes. Diabetes is a serious problem that could grow more serious in the future if people, health care systems, educational institutions, insurance companies, and the government don't act now.

Over the years there may have been some complacency, however the solution for complacency is a true sense of urgency. True urgency creates a level of determination for leaders to view a problem as an opportunity to use strategy to motivate people to change behavior and create heart- and mind-driven solutions.

As the diabetes population grows, there becomes a strategic need for increased awareness, engaged patient self-management, and the development of an effective approach to fight this life-threatening condition affecting our nation. Every strategic plan is driven by a mission and vision that provides core services to meet community health needs.

The American health care delivery system is evolving with many service innovations geared toward advancing chronic care. Hospital CEOs and presidents across the nation are recognizing diabetes as public health concern that requires immediate action. There is a sense urgency to translate strategy into actions. In Cleveland, Ohio, the need for action has elevated. Cleveland's population has an adult diabetes rate of 10 percent, which exceeds the 8 percent national average.

Gus Kious, the president of Huron Hospital, a Cleveland Clinic Hospital, recognized the sense of urgency and established a strategy to improve access to diabetes care and reduce health care disparities. Initiatives established to execute the strategy included increased diabetes awareness and access to care through population-based education and community outreach, multidisciplinary approach to care, patient self-management education, and an assessment tool to measure performance outcomes in the form of a scorecard. These initiatives provide the framework for the scorecard to measure how the initiatives create value for the customer, enhance internal capabilities, and improve future performance.

INCREASE DIABETES AWARENESS AND ACCESS TO CARE

In effort to educate the community regarding the proliferation and prevention of diabetes, a comprehensive Journey to Wellness program was established. The program offers a wide array of community outreach events that include:

- Health forums and talks
- A diabetes education TV channel within patient rooms 9999
- Fitness classes
- Diabetes support groups
- Twelve-step food addicts and overeaters programs
- Cooking classes
- Careers and volunteer opportunities
- Health wise connection tours
- Health screenings

Promoting early detection and timely treatment can help save lives. Health screenings assist in identifying people at risk for chronic diseases such as diabetes, kidney disease, and hypertension. Community outreach health screenings offer another access channel into the health care system.

More than one hundred free healthy heart screenings events are offered throughout the community in various locations ranging from churches, schools, senior citizens homes, local businesses, corporations, community recreation facilities, homeless shelters, barber shops, salons, and libraries. The healthy heart program provides screenings for blood sugar, blood pressure and cholesterol. Additional screenings for overweight, foot disease, and eye disease are provided. Over 2,500 people have been screened at these events on annual basis.

Community residents without a primary care physician who are participating in the screenings are also introduced to physicians during the outreach events. The Journey to Wellness program is another example of translating the strategy into action by increasing awareness and access to physician care by helping save lives, promoting disease prevention, and connecting patients with medical complications to the health care system.

To further increase awareness and improve access to diabetes care, the following actions were taken:

- The hospital offered financial counselors to the uninsured and underinsured with financial assistance.
- An endocrinology fellowship was established to expand physician coverage.
- Additional diabetes educators were hired for inpatient and outpatient services.
- Diabetes education services were expanded to satellite facilities in adjacent markets.
- Endocrinologists created new diabetes clinics within outpatient clinic and women's center.
- Over twelve thousand community residents received diabetes education material.

MULTIDISCIPLINARY APPROACH TO CARE

Patients with diabetes can have multiple acute and long-term complications that require a multidisciplinary approach to care. The complications can be related to co-morbidities such as hypertension, kidney failure, vascular disease, and heart failure.

My brother's co-morbidities were correlated to his heart attack, which led to his diabetes-related death in 2009. The death of a family member can inspire many to partner with family members and hospitals to create change.

To address these co-morbidities, I led the creation of a minority health resource center located with local community library and sponsored by the hospital. The new health resource center was established in 2009 and was the first of its kind in Ohio, and possibly in the nation.

The purpose of the innovative center was to improve access to health information and educate the community on diabetes and chronic diseases. Services in the library health resource center included access to dedicated health focused personal computers, health books, DVDs, health screenings, in-person physician presentations, and large TV monitors reporting upcoming health-related events within the community.

In addition I was responsible for partnering with the hospital to establish a clinical infrastructure and programs conveniently located in proximity to the diabetes education center. Services included a team of specialties such as primary care, endocrinology, cardiology, nephrology, podiatry, ophthalmology, and wound care. The endocrinologists collaborate with specialists to provide coordinated care, timely interventions, and effective clinical outcomes.

A team approach to care was essential; therefore the partnership established a chronic disease section comprised of physician medical directors and nurse-led kidney disease, cardiovascular disease, Coumadin, and diabetes education clinics. Access to the clinics are dependent upon physician referrals. The chronic disease clinic structure supports physicians and disease management and contributes to clinical interventions and improved outcomes.

PATIENT SELF-MANAGEMENT

Hospitals across the United States are developing diabetes education centers, hiring health educators, and adopting best practice models of care consistent with American Diabetes Association standards of medical care.

For example, many hospitals have internationally recognized diabetes education centers that are staffed with a program manager, certified diabetes educators, a disease management ambassador, receptionists, dieticians, and an endocrinologist who serves as medical director and outreach educator to physicians. Entry into the program is predicated on physician referral.

The program offers a comprehensive diabetes self-management program available to inpatients, outpatients, and the community on an individual or group class basis. The goal is to assist patients in gaining mind- and heart-driven confidence to make healthy lifestyle changes and learn self-management skills to control their diabetes and optimize their ability to live a productive and satisfying life.

The class curriculum involves various sessions, beginning with "getting started" concepts by accepting diabetes, understanding risk factors, and warnings, and establishing treatment plan. The next session deals with improving the quality of life through better self-management of diabetes. The third and fourth sessions address the challenge of sensible eating and getting regular exercise. The fifth and sixth sessions emphasize taking medications and testing your blood sugar. The final sessions cover diabetes self-management and complications that can happen.

The program has been a great success because the hospital has been able to report an annual increase in education class visits and favorable health outcomes that reduced A1C scores, inpatient length of stay, amputation rates, thirty-day readmission rates, and cost of care.

PERFORMANCE MEASUREMENT SCORECARD

The scorecard provides executives with a comprehensive framework to translate vision and diabetes strategies into sets of access, health outcome, and financial performance measures. It can be used to measure diabetes strategy, communicate outcomes, alignment with organizational vision, and translation of strategy into action.

The diabetes scorecard measures are separated into three categories: access, health outcome, and financial performance. Each measurement is compared to the performance of the previous year and the established target. The access category contained volume measurements such as number patients, outpatient visits, admissions, total encounters, and market share.

Health outcome measurements included A1C results, length of stay, amputations, mortality rates, number of diabetes education visits, total health screening events and people screened, case mix index, and thirty-day readmit rates. The financial metrics included net revenue and net revenue per case, direct cost and direct cost per case, and contribution margin.

SUMMARY

Twenty-four million Americans (8 percent) have diabetes, and another fifty-seven million people have elevated blood sugar called prediabetes. These startling statistics reflect the growing public health concern of diabetes and have created a sense of urgency to translate strategy into action. This sense of urgency is relevant in Cleveland and in Huron Hospital due to diabetes rate exceeding the national average.

The vision of the Huron Hospital president has empowered the Huron team to translate strategies into action to improve outcomes and access to care. Mr. Lawson was responsible for overseeing the initiatives that increased diabetes awareness and access to care, ensured multidisciplinary approach to care, supported the patient self-management program success, and communicated performance results of diabetes scored card.

The success of the strategies and actions resulted in additional strategic outcome such as:

- A 36 percent reduction in amputations from 2003 to 2009
- A length of stay reduction of 21.5 percent from 2003 to 2009
- An 11 percent growth in outpatient visits from 2007 to 2009
- Over 100 annual screening events and more than 2,000 people screened
- The number-one ranked local diabetes market share leader with 28 percent of market
- A 23 percent lower 30 day readmit rate for patients receiving diabetes education
- An annual cost savings of $432,000 due to fewer patients readmitted within 30 days
- An 8 percent increase in new patients choosing Huron from 2005 to 2008

CHAPTER FOURTEEN

CONCLUSIONS

In today's turbulent times, Americans and corporations are faced with overcoming personal and corporate finance problems, health crises, unemployment, and the need change behaviors and cultures in order to survive. Despite these challenges, there is hope and opportunities to turn around our situations.

Throughout history the average American and visionary leaders have demonstrated the ability to navigate through the turbulence and land safely and successfully in life.

For example, a single parent mother was able to overcome financial challenges and successfully raise her children to be healthy and productive citizens. Remember that Abraham Lincoln overcame poverty; the deaths of his mother, sister, and brother; and several political defeats to become president of the United States.

Leading change in turbulent times will always require an emergency and stabilization plan, understanding of the root cause of the problem, team effort, behavior modification, and resource support. We cannot do it alone. For example, if it is a health-related problem, you will need a treatment plan, a team of health professionals, a diagnosis of root cause, a change in your habits and behavior, and a health insurance resource.

There is a saying that states in order to make a change, it first starts with the man in the mirror. Regardless if you're the CEO of a major corporation, an entrepreneur, a teacher, a real estate agent, a physician, a health administrator, or a parent, change must first start with you.

If the economy is in a recession and, your profits are declining, personal savings are near zero, jobs are in jeopardy or eliminated, or patients dying due to advanced disease and delayed care, you must has have a vision, execute the plan, and take control of your own destiny to help yourself and others.

After your plan is developed and execution begins, remember there is a transition process that may be difficult; however, adapting and accepting reality are keys to success. There will be several phases of the transition process, so remained committed to your vision because your ship will finally overcome the turbulent waves and come in safely to shore.

Once the transition process is complete, there will be a realization that the culture you assessed is changing, and your visionary leadership is demonstrating a successful turnaround and a rebirth. You have recognized the sense of urgency to address the health crisis, improve the financial performance, renew your core, and focus on growth to begin the new life cycle.

The support of United States government and other organizational partnerships help overcome turbulent times. For example, health reform, financial regulation, and economic recovery will allow Americans, corporations, and the overall world to lead change in their turbulent times and land safely. American history and case studies have proven time and time again that this outcome is a fact; therefore do not despair and execute your plan.

MICHAEL S. LAWSON

Michael S. Lawson grew up in Cleveland, earned his undergraduate in liberal arts education at Baldwin Wallace College, and received his masters in business administration at Cleveland State University. He has more than twenty-five years of health care experience. He began his first corporate employment at General Electric as an operations intern during his sophomore year at Baldwin Wallace College. After the internship Lawson needed funding to continue his education, and he landed an entry level X-ray tech assistant position within radiology operations at the Cleveland Clinic in 1985.

He was responsible for performing X-rays on patients within cardiac intensive care units, managing the portable radiography operations, and working side by side with world-renown cardio thoracic surgeons, cardiologists, CICU nurses, and radiologists. Lawson completed his undergraduate and graduate business studies, as well as his clinical training at the Clinic.

He eventually transitioned from a clinical role into an administrative role and began to methodically work his way up through the management ranks into the executive ranks. He served as administrator for various clinical departments and worked closely with community, government, and business leaders to help improve access to medical care and community health.

He advanced to vice president level over key institutes and core service lines (cancer, emergency care, brain health, diabetes, and neurosurgery) across the Cleveland Clinic Health System within academic medical center setting. After five years in that role and fifteen years of management experience, Lawson had interest in becoming community hospital president, and he took a vice president of operation position at one of Cleveland Clinic's community hospitals that allowed him to back up the hospital president and learn the role.

Lawson was responsible for aiding the president, strategic planning, leading clinical and support service operations, monitoring construction projects, serving as hospital government and community relations liaison for the president, and assisting fund development and physician recruitment.

During his time at the Cleveland Clinic Health System, he led growth and turnaround of several business units and institutes, improved national cancer rankings, oversaw cost-reduction initiatives, supervised organizational restructuring and employee career developments, established new institutes and programs, developed new chronic disease and diabetes management programs, oversaw minority health initiatives, completed strategic plans to construct a new community health center and an innovative health resource center, and developed strategic community and business partnership to improve access to health care and funding.

Lawson has served on community development, health, and editorial boards. He has lectured at hospitals and local and national conferences. He has authored several management articles in national health management journals as well as co-authored clinical studies in minority health. He has turned around clinical operations, financial performances, and satisfaction scores and has helped improve community health and the culture of organizations.

In 2009 Lawson accepted a promotion at OhioHealth System, serving as senior vice president of operations, which is the chief operating officer role at one of the health system's high-performing hospitals. Lawson continues his commitment to strategic integration, improving community health, access to care, and hospital turnarounds.

Lawson serves as a board member of number-one ranked and nationally recognized Columbus Metropolitan Library, and he enjoys research and writing, reading, and fitness.

Made in the USA
Coppell, TX
30 November 2024

41394397R00065